School-based curriculum development in Britain

Routledge Education Books

Advisory editor: John Eggleston
Professor of Education
University of Keele

School-based curriculum development in Britain

A collection of case studies

Edited by
John Eggleston

Routledge & Kegan Paul
London, Boston and Henley

First published in 1980
by Routledge & Kegan Paul Ltd
39 Store Street, London WC1E 7DD,
9 Park Street,
Boston, Mass 02108, USA
and Broadway House, Newtown Road,
Henley-on-Thames, Oxon RG9 1EN
Set in IBM Press Roman by
Hope Services, Abingdon, Oxon
and printed in Great Britain by
Redwood Burn Ltd
Trowbridge & Esher
editorial selection, Editor's preface and Introduction
© John Eggleston 1980;
articles © Routledge & Kegan Paul 1980

British Library Cataloguing in Publication Data

School-based curriculum development
in Britain. – (Routledge education
books).
1. Curriculum planning – Great Britain
– Case studies
I. Eggleston, John
375'.001'0722   LB1564.G7   80-40020

ISBN 0 7100 0446 X

Contents

Notes on contributors   vii
Editor's preface   ix
Introduction   1
John Eggleston

1 The Independent Learning in Science model of school-based   14
curriculum development
Eric L. Green
2 Children Investigating and teachers writing   41
Ken Wild
3 Continuing curriculum change at Codsall School   57
Paul Abbs
4 Curriculum development and staff development at the   97
Abraham Moss Centre
Ron Mitson
5 The development of a Humanities curriculum at   116
Manor Park School
Patrick Eavis
6 Language through the curriculum at Hele's School   134
Peter Cloke

Index   145

Notes on contributors

Paul Abbs is Director of Studies at Codsall High School, Wolverhampton

Peter Cloke is Head of English at Hele's School, Exeter

Patrick Eavis is Headmaster of Manor Park School, Newcastle upon Tyne

John Eggleston is Professor and Head of the Department of Education at Keele University

Eric L. Green is Secretary of the Independent Learning in Science Project and Head of the Physical Science Department at Countesthorpe College

Ron Mitson is Principal of the Abraham Moss Centre, Manchester

Ken Wild is Advisory Officer, Staffordshire Local Education Authority

Editor's preface

School-based curriculum development has, in the early 1980s, become the dominant form of the curriculum development movement. After a decade in which the main effort has been focused on the national project, we have come slowly to realise that if change in the schools is the objective, then the initiative must also come from the schools. The result has been a gradual resurgence of curriculum development that arises directly from the needs and enthusiasms of the schools, their pupils and their teachers. Some large schools have undertaken their own programmes, often with impressive results. Others have joined forces, sharing common needs and enjoying common achievements. Still others have found that new-style national projects have provided an opportunity for genuine in-school iniatives of a highly effective nature.

No doubt we shall ultimately evolve sophisticated strategies of school-based curriculum development; curriculum theorists will produce comprehensive analyses of the process. The Schools and In-Service Teacher Education Evaluation Project and many other inquiries will throw new light upon events. But there is also a clear and immediate need to provide information on the way that school-based curriculum development is actually happening so that other schools may benefit, so that teachers may be more fully able to participate and so that students may be better prepared for this new and important extension of the professional role.

This volume presents six case studies of a variety of forms of development in the schools. Each shows not only the development of curriculum but also the staffing and administrative implications that arise. Following an editorial introduction, there are accounts of school-based developments at Codsall, Staffordshire; Manor Park, Newcastle; Abraham Moss Centre, Manchester; and Hele's School, Exeter. There are also studies of the in-school and inter-school activities in the Independent Learning in Science Project and in the Nuffield Integrated Science Project.

Preface

The authors of the case studies join me in expressing our warm appreciation of the many colleagues in and around our institutions who have co-operated in the developments reported and also in the reporting of them. School-based curriculum development, like all grass-roots democratic movements, is heavily, and properly, labour intensive. Our thanks also go to Mary McBratney for assembling and typing the manuscript, to the Keele Education Library for consistent help in providing and checking source material, and to David Godwin of Routledge & Kegan Paul for his encouragement of the project. I am also personally grateful to members of the Centre for Educational Research and Innovation, OECD, Paris, for their early initiative in alerting me more fully to the importance of this field by inviting me to produce a working paper for them.

John Eggleston

Introduction

John Eggleston

The curriculum has always been the key to what happens in schools. It is the device through which the vast range of knowledge and values, skills and roles which the school offers to its pupils, is organised, taught and eventually evaluated. For this reason if no other, there has always been curriculum development as knowledge has changed, methodology has advanced and the results of our efforts have illuminated our practice. Although we value tradition, often highly, there is hardly a single component of the curricula of our schools in the 1980s that bears meaningful relationship with the curricula of 1880. Some landmarks, notably textbooks, survive for many years. Generations are familiar with Durrell's Arithmetic or Ridout's English. But in the long run all is change; there is little that is absolute in the curriculum, most is relative, much of it surprisingly so.

Unquestionably the greatest part of this change has originated in the schools themselves as teachers have adapted, adjusted and interpreted the conditions that they find – both outside the school and inside their own classrooms.

If this is the case, then wherein lies the novelty of school-based curriculum development? In one sense such development is certainly not new! It is no more than a re-expression of the prevailing norms. But in another sense it is wholly new, for it represents a take-over by the schools of the new active rather than passive style of curriculum change. For generations the curriculum developed slowly and imperceptibly. It was no teacher's specific task to take hold of it and set out to change it. Though the 'great educators' such as Rousseau, Dewey, Pestalozzi, Neill and a handful of others applied some powerful pressures from time to time, their intervention was, at best, limited and spasmodic; in no way did it constitute a concerted, planned strategy of curriculum change.

It is just this concerted, planned strategy of change that has characterised the past two decades in Britain and in many other countries.

1

Curriculum development has been transformed into an active rather than a passive form, explicit rather than implicit in its strategies and public rather than private in its affairs.

There are many reasons for these changes. Perhaps the most obvious has been the rapidity of social change to which the curriculum must respond. The curriculum in mathematics changes in an age of computerisation; the curriculum in science responds to the age of electronics. The new media of communication make changes in language studies inescapable. Changing social attitudes and values affect not only the motivations and values of students in the schools but also their response to curriculum.

Another set of factors has been the major reorganisation of schooling itself. Both at primary and secondary level fundamental changes in the nature and distribution of the school population have made new patterns of curriculum imperative. Such changes have included the raising of the school leaving age, comprehensive reorganisation, the introduction of mixed-ability teaching, project work, integrated days, individualised learning, new examinations and assessment systems. Each calls for major adjustments in curriculum organisation and methodology.

Yet a further group of reasons concern the growing pressures upon schools and teachers to be accountable. Such pressures call upon teachers to explain and justify the learning experiences they offer in a manner that was seldom if ever required in the past. Changes in the curriculum accelerate such demands; parents and employers are far more likely to ask teachers to account for curricula that are different from those that they themselves experienced when at school. In order to respond to such demands, teachers find it increasingly necessary to acquire a new professional capacity, the use of what Sharp and Green[1] call an 'accounting language'. Their book vividly illustrates the problems of 'Mrs Carpenter' and her colleagues who appear to lack this capacity.

National curriculum development projects

The imperatives of such changes led almost inescapably to a new and revolutionary device: the national curriculum development project. The new approach was pioneered in Britain by the Nuffield Foundation in its attempts to bring about radical developments in science education — to close the gap between the practice of science in the community and that in the school curriculum. But the work of the Nuffield Foundation, though substantial, was still small in comparison to the subsequent activity of the Schools Council. A national body supported by central and local government, the Council had, as one of its two main purposes, the development of curriculum in the schools of England and Wales (the other closely related purpose being the development of examinations). The work of the Foundation, the Council, and a range of other national bodies spread rapidly through the 1960s and in a decade became an established part of the educational life of England, Wales, Scotland and Northern Ireland. The period has been documented extensively;[2] the successes and failures of the movement are a perennial subject for debate. But the essential feature of the whole movement was the belief that curriculum development could and would become a planned and rational activity. The objectives of the various areas of the curriculum were to be identified through consultation, consensus upon them reached, appropriate methodologies and contents identified, and these objectives were to be achieved in the classrooms. Subsequently, this model came to be augmented by a feedback process of evaluation that allowed its continuing adaptation in the light of such illumination.

In retrospect, this simple logic can be seen to be naive and even unrealistic in the complex and changing world inhabited by schools and their students. Perhaps its greatest error was to take insufficient account of the long-standing school-based tradition of curriculum development. This was seen very clearly in many evaluations of projects, notably that conducted by Shipman, Bolam and Jenkins of the Schools Council Integrated Studies Project.[3] This showed a disparity, at times remarkable, between the expectations of the project organisers and the achievements in the schools. Even in the trial schools, in which the national team worked extensively, the use made by individual teachers of the project materials was spontaneous and largely unpredictable by the central team. Overall the usage was far less than that which the team believed to be the case; the materials were certainly used when the team was present but far less when they were not. Even the declared enthusiasm of Heads to adopt the material in their schools was by no means always put into practice.

It is easy to suggest that these disparities arose due to teacher hostility or indifference. But the evidence does not support this view. Rather it appears that the teachers have an accurate knowledge of the needs of their children, the resources available to them and their own personal capacities, which is far more up to date and sensitive than that of 'outsiders' can ever be. In the light of such evidence, the materials being produced by national projects came to be seen not so much as ready-made curricula; instead they were to be seen as an addition to the resources at the disposal of teachers to use as and when appropriate in the light of their professional judgment.

The resources movement

If the national development project was the mode of the late 1960s, then the resources movement was that of the early 1970s. Even before the large projects produced their materials, the concept of learning resources in both primary and secondary schools had developed rapidly in response to the adoption of mixed-ability teaching and individualised learning. Schools found it imperative to build up good collections of books, maps, periodicals, and a wide range of unbound material including press cuttings, handouts and other documents. Indeed, many of the major projects such as the Schools Council/Nuffield Humanities Projects produced almost all of their project materials in 'packs' rather than in conventional book form. It was also necessary to establish stocks of audio-visual materials such as slide-tape packages and multi-media kits — the software for language laboratories and much else.

Many schools established and staffed resource centres; an early pioneer was Codsall School (the basis of one of the case studies later in this volume) which set up its centre because national curriculum projects 'often left the teacher more frustrated in that he was unable to continue and develop the work in his own school, through lack of materials and facilities to be creative and the opportunities to use his real professional skills'.[4]

So great was the movement that the Schools Council itself established the Resource Centre Project based at the University of London Institute of Education. Its stated objective clearly displays the move from project-focused to school-focused initiatives that was taking place. It was

> to identify various problems which faced schools and authorities wishing to develop resource centres, and to determine what has so far been found to be the most suitable and practicable methods of solving them, having regard to a wide variety of existing conditions. Special attention will be paid to indexing, storage and retrieval systems.[5]

The Nuffield Foundation too adopted parallel strategies establishing its own Resources for Learning Project, examining how the resources available to schools might most profitably be used. A number of Nuffield Resources for Learning Development Units were established in different parts of the country.

School based in-service training

Yet another step in the move to take the action back into the schools has been the development of in-service education and training. Like curriculum development, in-service training was originally conceived as a largely external strategy whereby teachers could be helped to develop not only their curricula but also their organisation, pastoral care, and many other aspects of schooling. Yet in the 1970s it became equally clear that very much in-service training could be better placed in the school itself rather than in the colleges or even the teachers' centres. Partington of Waltham Forest Local Education Authority wrote:

> There will remain an important INSET role for University and College based secondments and for shorter courses in Teachers' Centres or Professional Centres, but I am convinced that a major change of emphasis to school-focused activities is necessary if a major advance is to take place both in the personal development of teachers and in the effectiveness of their professional work.[6]

Such developments were certainly encouraged by the James Report advocacy of a widespread expansion of in-service teacher training. One of the recommendations reads:

> Every school should have on its staff a 'professional tutor' to co-ordinate second and third cycle work affecting the school and to be the link between the school and other agencies engaged in that work. Whether the professional tutor were the head or deputy head, as might be the case in a small school or a designated member of the staff in a larger school, it would be important for all teachers designated as professional tutors to be among the first to be admitted to third cycle courses, so that they could be trained for their new tasks. Among the responsibilities of a professional tutor would be that of compiling and maintaining a training programme for the staff of the school, which would take account both of the curricular needs of the school and of the professional needs of the teachers.[7]

The enhanced commitment of teachers in in-service training taking place in their own school is strikingly illustrated by Bolam, currently Director of a Department of Education and Science sponsored project: The Schools and In-Service Teacher Education Evaluation Project. He writes of one school:

> At the Castle School, these conferences have lasted for one to two days and have usually taken the form of guest speaker lectures and small discussion groups. The first conference arose because the school was going comprehensive and some staff felt the need to prepare for the change in this way. Subsequently conferences were planned by the working parties. . . .

The figures presented by Bolam:

> provide striking evidence of the relative attractiveness of a conference which is based at the school and is exclusively for school staff. Over 90% of the staff attended two such conferences but their attendance dropped dramatically when the venue was changed and the conference was opened to staff from other schools.[8]

Introduction

The Department of Education and Science discussion paper *Making INSET Work,*[9] published in November 1978, contains strong support for school based in-service work in the curriculum and other areas. Addressed to teachers, the paper argues:

> INSET is particularly important at the present time. Society is changing faster than ever and is making increasingly complex demands upon schools. Teachers are having to introduce changes in school structures and curricula. Falling school rolls are causing new problems, including reduced promotion possibilities for teachers. If they are to respond positively to these and similar pressures, teachers will need access to good facilities.

The paper goes on to suggest:

> that the process starts in your school. What are the problems which face the school from day to day, and from year to year, in its curricula, its organisation and methods? What are the aspects of the work in your classroom or with teaching groups about which you are not entirely happy, or the new problems which arise and which you would like to solve? These are the issues which you as a teacher and you and your colleagues together as a school staff can and should examine regularly and consider how they might best be tackled. This is where INSET may help — that is to say INSET arising out of and designed to meet your particular circumstances, whether by planned discussions in school perhaps with outside help, by visits to other schools or centres, or for some by personal secondment and appropriate courses.

The re-birth of school-based curriculum development

The curriculum development movement, the resources movement and the school-based in-service training movement, came together in the resurgence of school-based curriculum development in the mid 1970s. The fusion was perhaps most clearly spelt out in the Schools Council Report, *The Whole Curriculum,*[10] which stated:

> we want to highlight what we see as being the key concepts in our report. Among the most important of these is the idea of the school as a centre of curriculum development. We believe the improvement of the secondary school curriculum must rest upon an acknowledgement of the central role of the teacher. All worthwhile proposals for curriculum change are put to the test in classrooms and only come to fruition if the practising teacher has the resources, support, training and self-confidence to implement them. Teachers are in a unique position to know and understand the needs of pupils and

6

from them should come the principal pressure for increasingly effective programmes of teaching and learning. Because we see the development of the curriculum and the self-development of the teacher as being inseparable, we call for vigorous programmes of in-service education and school-based curriculum development, both of which are essential if the teachers are to perform their role to the full.

How may we define this reborn school-based curriculum development? It is essentially a process in which the detailed strategies for a curriculum appropriate to the needs of the individual children in the specific school, or even in the specific unit of a school, are developed by co-operative discussion, planning, trial and evaluation. It is a process that may be aided by a planned utilisation of the resources of the school; its human resources and those that spring from its architecture and location as well as its access to materials developed by national and regional curriculum development agencies, commercial bodies and the initiatives of local and central government. It is a process that reflects the assets and liabilities both of the school and the community it serves. It is certainly a process that responds to the challenge experienced in many schools to provide a curriculum that motivates and involves pupils and that also encourages the teachers to give of their best. Above all else, it is a curriculum that is achieved by the school rather than ascribed to it. In short, it is a dynamic element within the school that has largely been created therein and for which the school is collectively responsible. It is an instrument for which the school is accountable and through which the school may accept accountability.

The sequence of events that has been described suggests that school-based curriculum development should now exist in almost every school. Yet, though widespread, school-based curriculum development is by no means universal. In some schools it does not exist at all, in others it is at best rare and spasmodic. Clearly there are some schools where size, acute staff shortage and other special factors present major impediments. But apart from these, what are the conditions in which school-based curriculum development appears to prosper?

Perhaps the most notable feature is a 'readiness' — a stage in the development of the thinking of the staff at which the need for school-based curriculum development becomes clearly evident. This condition is well put by Forward, Headmaster of a junior school in which school-based curriculum development occurred early:

> To achieve the goals we had set ourselves demanded considerable alteration to the curriculum and organization of the school. As we worked ourselves towards a viable organization and curriculum through team discussion and classroom innovation a number of demands and restraints began to emerge.

The demand which seemed to us to be central to the achievement of our goals was the need to individualize the work of the children as much as possible. If we were to base our teaching on the needs of the child then our first task must be to get to know the children well — and if we were to answer personal and social needs as well as academic needs then we had to get to know the children as people, not merely as scholars. This translated itself into the need for a teacher to work with individual children often alone but also in small groups. This called for a flexibility of grouping which one teacher alone in the enclosed classroom was unlikely to achieve. Thus flexibility was a prerequisite.

The need for flexible grouping was also echoed in another demand. The creation of proper interests and enthusiasms was to be one of our goals. The ability to group children with others pursuing the same interest demanded that we be able to create groups from a wide selection of children more perhaps than one would find within one classroom.

The ability to respond to varying needs in the classroom also demanded a wide range of skills and interests in the teacher. The question arose as to whether as the children grew older one teacher could assemble all those skills and interests.[11]

But such a need must not only exist; teachers must recognise that it exists and be ready to respond to it. We have already emphasised the autonomy of teachers in England and Wales: autonomous teachers may well be encouraged and even inspired to participate in school-based curriculum development, they cannot be forced to do so. There is also little doubt that their enthusiasm may be reinforced if they see that adequate support — administrative, material and moral — is available. Good resources, adequate professional and non-professional staffing and sympathetic leadership inside and outside the school seem to be important concomitants of enduring school-based curriculum development.

The needs of parents are also important. Holt,[12] writing of school-based curriculum development in a comprehensive school, is alert to the issue of accountability. He comments:

> Right from the start, then, it was clear that if new departures were to be made in the school's curriculum, it would be essential not only to explain them to future parents but also to try to convince them that, bluntly, the risk in sending their children to a school with new ideas was worth taking.

Parental support may also be useful in the practical implementation of school-based curriculum development. Recently a comprehensive school instituted a resource preparation room as part of its school-based curriculum development programme. The poor acoustic qualities of the only room available presented serious difficulties in the preparation of audio resources. On hearing of this difficulty, the parents' association, already in sympathy with the scheme, raised funds to enable the room to be fitted with carpeting and acoustic panelling.

But it is not only the positive aspects of readiness for school-based curriculum development that require consideration. We must also consider the many aspects of a school that may make it less than ready — or which may even impede the process of school-based curriculum development once it has begun. Skilbeck[13] has listed a number of factors that may cause difficulties in school-based curriculum development. They include:

1   A sense of low self-esteem and inadequacy in staff, and lack of relevant skills, e.g. in analysing objectives, constructing tests, working in planning groups, etc.; failure of authorities to provide advisory and specialist consultancy services.
2   Lack of interest or conviction in staff, particularly in sustaining change processes over a period of time; careful planning is hard work.
3   Inadequate allocations of resources (time and personnel as well as money); rigidity and bureaucracy in control of resources.
4   Conflicting priorities on part of teacher, e.g. planning, teaching, assessing, private study, increased leisure and recreational interests; lack of incentive to teachers to engage in planning and evaluation.
5   Rapid staff turnover.
6   Reconciling what may be conflicting demands e.g. official requirements, external examination, parental pressures, pupil interests, teachers' educational values.
7   Inadequacy of theoretical models — teachers tend to reject what they cannot readily apply.
8   Complexity of issues and of managerial problems e.g. designing and implementing individual study programmes within a common core curriculum.
9   Failure to appreciate subtleties of group interactions when the balance of power in an existing institution is threatened.
10   Tendency of institutions to revert to earlier forms of organization and control if the pressure for change is not continuous.
11   Discontinuance of new practices before they have been fully implemented and diffused.

Overall, it is clear that the enthusiasm of the individual teacher, his involvement and readiness are central. Not only are such personal characteristics necessary to ensure an adequate level of individual participation but also the degree of collective responsibility that is accepted and 'internalised' by the individual rather than being attributed to 'them'. This is by no means yet another idealist prescription. In the realities of school life the motivation of the teacher may spring not only from lofty pedagogical principle but also imperative self-interest. The urgency of a solution to new and pressing problems in the classroom or even the quest for personal survival may well lie at the heart of some of the most successful school-based curriculum development programmes.

The case studies

The six case studies that constitute the remainder of this volume abundantly satisfy the criteria that have been listed for effective and soundly based school-based curriculum development. Two are accounts of 'collective action' where work by teachers in a number of schools is brought together to solve problems common to all the schools. The remaining studies are accounts of work wholly undertaken for and within the schools concerned — though often enlisting considerable outside assistance.

The two accounts of 'collective action' are both responses to the problems experienced by schools in the teaching of 'new science' with its strong emphases on individualised experimentation and learning. The chapter by Green describes the Independent Learning in Science organisation, a grass-roots body set up by a number of science teachers faced with the task of assisting children of a wide range of abilities to undertake the independent learning activities required by the new science curricula. The development of the organisation, the commitment of its members and the effective strategies devised in the participating schools are clearly documented.

Wild offers a closely related account of two activities also designed to help pupils to respond more fully to the new science. The strategy adopted was to produce booklets for use in the schools that made the new approaches more accessible and comprehensible to their specific groups of pupils. The first activity took place in Staffordshire schools where teachers produced a set of booklets to help children working with the Science 5–13 Project and similar programmes. The second activity involved a wider group of teachers preparing booklets for another national project — the Nuffield Integrated Science Project — this time working mainly within rather than outside the organisation of the project. Indeed, as Wild makes clear, the success of the first activity was a major factor in the decision to build a new national project largely around this mode of operation.

The first of the 'single school' case studies is of Codsall School,

Staffordshire, one of the pioneering schools in the development of a resource centre, in-service training and school-based curriculum development. Here Abbs, Director of Studies, gives perhaps the most detailed account yet published of the way a school has developed its whole organisation around its resource centre to form a comprehensive instrument of school-based curriculum development. Abbs presents a wide range of information on the staffing arrangements, course provision, resource organisation and evaluation at Codsall that will be of the greatest value to all readers.

Mitson, himself previously Head of Codsall, follows with an account of work at the Abraham Moss Centre, Manchester — an innovative educational complex where the school is part of a major development in community provision. Mitson describes a sophisticated system of school-based in-service training that is being used to generate the special curricular approaches adopted at Abraham Moss Centre. The chapter is a frank account of its successes and its failures:

> The development of Core Studies by our first Curriculum Consultative Committee captured the imagination of the majority of staff and filled the school with a professional concern and commitment unrivalled by any institution. Despite the momentum created by this, putting the ideas into practice proved to be an enormous burden for the members of a single school staff to shoulder. Eventually the demands of those studies outside the Cores had to be fulfilled also, work on some of the more exciting developments had to be shelved, and the frustration of not being able to continue the work bit deep. The self-contained courses for our fifteen and sixteen year olds will take many years to establish for the same reason.

As with the previous chapter, readers will find the wealth of detail on staff training, course organisation and content to be of the greatest value.

Eavis, Headmaster of Manor Park School, Newcastle, offers an account of a more limited but no less important activity, the establishment of a Humanities curriculum. His record of how the specific need was identified, the fundamental changes that were put in train to accomplish it and the eventual success of the enterprise, testifies to the capacity of school-based curriculum development to achieve striking changes in the life of a school and the experience of its students.

In the final chapter Cloke describes two projects at Hele's school — an old-established grammar school in transition to an 11–16 comprehensive. The first was a response to the language problem being encountered by many 'new' pupils — problems in both spoken and written language. The second was an attempt to reduce the incidence of underachievement — a significant section of pupils were seen to be 'failing to do as well as had been hoped'. The identification of these problems by the school staff led the teachers to undertake research to innovate and eventually to publish in a way that not only enabled them to move closer to a solution to both problems, but also had a profound effect upon the *raison d'être* of the school itself.

Though widely differing in style, range and purpose, the six case studies have common elements that adequately justify their inclusion in a volume devoted to the furtherance of school-based curriculum development. All arose from clearly identified needs of the schools themselves; all derive their motive power from the enthusiasms of the teachers and all have the essential component of evaluation — formal and informal — that constitutes the key to successful development, changing it from an intermittent gamble to a continuous, rational process that is responsive, dynamic and accountable.

Yet such rewards are not easily achieved, as the case studies make clear. As Skilbeck[14] has noted, 'The task is complex and difficult for all concerned. It requires a range of cognitive skills, strong motivation, postponement of immediate satisfaction, constructive interactions in planning groups and emotional maturity.' But against Skilbeck's caution we may juxtapose Forward's[15] cautious optimism.

> The effect of being involved at first hand in decision making, the opportunity for continuing professional discussion over shared problems and, as a team, having an important part in the making of school educational policy has enabled even the youngest and the newest member of staff to be significant in the corporate life of the school.

He concludes, 'If living by consensus decision, consultation and professional discussion is at times an exhausting process, it is also a stimulating and very satisfying one.'

Forward's conclusion is one which the authors of this volume, emerging from their own collective and exhausting labours, warmly and enthusiastically endorse.

Notes

1   R. Sharp and A. G. Green, *Education and Social Control,* London, Routledge & Kegan Paul, 1976.

2   J. Eggleston, *The Sociology of the School Curriculum,* London, Routledge & Kegan Paul, 1976.

3   M. D. Shipman, D. Bolam and D. Jenkins, *Inside a Curriculum Project,* London, Methuen, 1974.

4   M. Holder and E. Hewton, 'A school resource centre', *British Journal of Educational Technology,* vol. 4, January 1973, p. 1.

5   N. W. Beswick, *School Resource Centres,* Schools Council Working Paper 43, London, Evans/Methuen, 1972.

6 G. Partington, 'School-focused INSET', *British Journal of In-Service Education,* vol. 3, no. 1, 1976, pp. 35–9.

7 Department of Education and Science, *Teacher Education and Training,* a report by a Committee of Inquiry appointed by the Secretary of State for Education and Science, under the Chairmanship of Lord James of Rusholme, London, HMSO, 1972.

8 R. Bolam, 'Innovation and the problem-solving school', in E. King (ed.), *Re-organising Education: Management and Participation for Change,* London, Sage, 1977.

9 Department of Education and Science, *Making INSET Work,* London, HMSO, 1978.

10 Schools Council, *The Whole Curriculum 13–16: Working Paper 53,* London, Evans/Methuen, 1975.

11 R. W. Forward, 'A time for change', in J. Walton and J. Welton (eds), *Rational Curriculum Planning,* London, Ward Lock, 1976.

12 M. J. Holt, 'Curriculum development at Sheredes School', in Walton and Welton (eds), op. cit.

13 M. Skilbeck, 'School-based curriculum development', in Walton and Welton (eds), op. cit.

14 M. Skilbeck, 'School Based Curriculum Development', mimeo, unpublished, Coleraine, University of Ulster, 1972.

15 Forward, op. cit.

Chapter 1

The Independent Learning in Science model of school-based curriculum development

Eric L. Green

For over a decade now, science teachers in the United Kingdom have been experimenting with a variety of schemes of independent learning, initiated by themselves with the intention of improving the quality of learning of their students. In part, this kind of development has occurred in science teaching in response to the emergence of inquiry-based curricula, which to many science teachers implies independent learning, that is, schemes of work differentiated according to the age, ability and aptitude of individual students. In part, the improved provision of educational technology in schools and/or at local teachers' centres has made the provision of suitable resources for independent learning easier, and has therefore contributed to the establishment of such learning schemes in schools. A further contribution to this process is the arrival of the unstreamed class, where traditional class teaching is seen to be inappropriate, but there is also evidence[1] that many teachers involved with streamed classes see the methods of independent learning as more appropriate to the needs of their students than traditional methods.

Initially, this movement to independent learning in science was virtually unrecognised, certainly having no formal organisational structure, and consisted of essentially randomly dispersed operations by individual science teachers. Early methods put considerable emphasis on an individualised approach,[2] and there were clear links, at that time, with the ideas and methods of programmed learning.[3] A marked increase in the reporting of these experiments, in the literature of science education, suggested the need for a formal professional group which could collect, collate and disseminate examples of good practice, and perhaps assist the improvement of that practice.[4] It was in this context, and as a result of informal discussions among science teachers involved in this kind of work, that the conference 'Individual and Small Group Methods in the Teaching of Science' was held at Countesthorpe College, in April 1973.[5] To the surprise of the organisers, over one hundred school and

14

university teachers, inspectors, advisers and publishers took part, clearly indicating that the time was ripe for such a conference to be held. The meeting provided a stimulating opportunity for consultation, confirmation, exploration and elaboration of ideas and methods, and in hindsight proved an important watershed for those involved in the school-based development of independent learning in science. There was an immediate recognition of mutual interests and the need for a supportive professional organisation of like-minded practitioners, with the result that, towards the end of the conference, the ILIS organisation was founded. The establishment of the organisation was considered vitally important at the time, and there is no doubt that it has played an essential supportive and developmental role in the creation of independent learning in science in schools. By the manner in which the ILIS organisation functions, it represents a novel emphasis in curriculum development, certainly in science education, and one which it is felt is particularly congruent with the school-based curriculum development. The central organisation, through its officers and publications,[6] is not a curriculum writing and development team, but provides the vital supportive, co-ordinating and promotional link between teachers in schools.

> The local, school-based groups should be seen as the engine-room of the development. It should be clear to all science teachers that all local groups are open to access by anyone with interest or ideas. It is, I believe, essential to the success of such a learning scheme that the individual teacher should be able to take a very active role in devising his own scheme, based on these resources, and not merely a passive agent doling out the prescribed materials.[7]

It is believed that the ILIS organisation provides an important model for school-based curriculum development, and it is suggested that its methods and structure might be imitated in many other areas of the curriculum. Curriculum development in the individual school is the vital and fundamental requirement of curriculum change, but in isolation fails to disperse its achievements, tends to neglect similar experiences of others which might otherwise be extremely useful, and misses out on that corporate spirit of endeavour which illuminates the horizons and carries one through the difficult and frustrating periods of curriculum change. This model carries with it many important implications – the co-ordinating role of the central organisation, development of local workshop/resource centres, in-school training, in-service training, communications between teachers, teacher participation – and it is hoped that these factors will become quite explicit as the description of the ILIS organisation is developed. Members themselves, of course, have a continuing dialogue about such matters.

There is one feature of this model which is worth special consideration

15

at this point. Curriculum development in science education has, so far, been largely dominated by the centralised curriculum development team, producing materials, essentially in isolation from the schools, which, it is hoped, grateful teachers will accept. Like other, well-known, tablets of stone, such statements are frequently rejected. The 'mountain top' type curriculum development, however inspired, must inevitably have such a consequence, because of its lack of grass-roots consultation and participation. It surely was not surprising that the Schools Council funded a project to look into the uptake of its own projects – a matter which has given some cause for concern. ILIS is an organisation involved with decentralised curriculum development, disseminating its ideas and resources by a diffusion process, uptake being primarily dependent on teacher/teacher contact. For example, the Nuffield A-Level Physics Independent Learning Resources were first developed and used at Countesthorpe College, but are now in use at some twenty-five other educational institutions and interest continues to grow. The ILIS organisation exists to facilitate this diffusion process, considering it an important element in school-based curriculum development. Such a process has important implications, not least of which is its cost-effectiveness in supporting teachers in initiating curriculum change in their schools. A large print order is never required, schools sending out copies of their original materials when requested, usually at cost. ILIS is essentially a teachers' co-operative.

It is important, now, to consider the intentions and practices of the ILIS organisation in some detail so that its significance for teachers involved in school-based curriculum development may be better understood.

Aims of the ILIS organisation

Aim I To provide co-ordination of thought and enterprise in establishing methods of independent learning in science, the main interest, at present, being in the secondary school.

Aim II To provide for co-operative development in the preparation and dissemination of ideas and resources, primarily through local workshop and resource centres.

In elaborating on the aims of the ILIS organisation, it is intended to show that it exists to promote a process consistent in intention with the most informed thinking on localised curriculum development, principally represented by that of the Schools Council.[8] In other words, it is suggested that the ILIS type development is essentially in the mainstream of current educational thinking and a direct and important expression of it, albeit with significant contributions of its own to that thinking.

The essential elements of the process which the ILIS organisation exists to promote are:

> The careful examination, drawing on all available sources of knowledge and informed judgement, of the objectives of teaching . . . The object is to help as many teachers as possible to define, co-operatively, and from personal conviction, these objectives.
>
> The development and trial use in schools, of those methods and materials which are judged most likely to achieve the objectives which teachers agree upon.

The ILIS organisation also concurs with the Schools Council's basis for curriculum development in that, first, the ILIS model rests on a keen interest on the part of teachers in curricular progress. Groups of science teachers in ILIS are meeting to discuss curriculum problems and Local Education Authorities are making contributions to encourage such groups, in particular helping with such accommodation, apparatus and secretarial assistance as may be necessary.[9] Second, ILIS encourages Local Education Authorities, either singly or in collaboration with neighbouring Authorities, to consider ways of responding to the expressed wish of teachers to come together to conduct for themselves curriculum development, in order to sharpen their judgments on objectives, improve their experimental procedures and play a full part in assessing the results of development work. Third, the essence in the ILIS programme of curricular review and development is new thinking by the teachers themselves, as well as the appraisal of the thinking of others. This means that ILIS creates regular opportunities to meet together, both nationally and locally, and looks upon the initiation of thought, as well as the trial and assessment of new ideas and procedures drawn from other sources, as an integral part of its professional service to society. Within this context, the local ILIS workshop/resource centres have developed in a manner consistent with the suggested functions of such groups as described by the Schools Council,[10] viz:

> The most important function is to focus local interest and to give teachers a setting within which new objectives can be discussed and defined, and new ideas on content and method can be aired. The comments and criticism of local teachers show very clearly whether an idea which works well in one school can succeed in another. Teachers working in these local ILIS groups often seek a wider forum by invoking the help of the local authority or institute of education or both.[11]
>
> The schools in the area of the local workshop group are usually

among those who give new materials their trials. The local centre of interest contributes to the evaluation of materials, providing feedback comment, criticisms and suggestions for improvement directly to the curriculum developers.[12]

The local ILIS groups are kept informed about research and development in progress elsewhere. This is one of the important functions of the ILIS publications and part of the role of the officers of the organisation.

It is suggested then, that the aims of the ILIS organisation are firmly rooted in accepted educational thought about school-based curriculum development, and that the ILIS model, based on these aims, and now into its sixth year of development, ought to be further researched and evaluated so as to further inform teachers involved in similar school-based developments. As a first step in that process of research and evaluation, it is now intended to examine in some detail how the aims outlined above have affected the intentions and practices of science teachers in schools.

Aims of the teachers within the ILIS organisation

The emphasis in ILIS has, from the start, been the provision of assistance to teachers in building up their own approach to independent learning. This is considered a better approach to curriculum development than the centralised curriculum development of the last ten years or so, and probably more appropriate for changing the methods of learning/teaching. The intention of ILIS is to begin where the teacher is at, slowly assisting a change of perspective on learning, assisting in the development of new skills and resources, and encouraging the teacher to communicate his own learning to others attempting similar developments. Typical of the ILIS approach to the teacher fresh to independent learning, would be the suggestion that perhaps only some of the work, initially anyway, should be along these lines, the bulk of it being in the style which is well established and in which the teacher concerned has confidence. Once the teacher has experienced fruitful experiment in a limited trial of independent learning with his students, then he will extend his horizons based on the confidence engendered by the small-scale trial. He may of course reject this approach to learning. At no time has the ILIS organisation suggested that there is such a thing as THE method of independent learning; in fact, on the contrary, it has indicated that there are many varieties of approach flexible to the skills and interests of the individual teacher. The view is taken that these skills and interests should represent a major input into any independent learning scheme devised — a sharp contrast with the implications of centralised curriculum development.

There are, of course, many similarities in the variety of approaches developed, providing therefore the *raison d'être* of the ILIS organisation.

What is it that makes teachers want to experiment with the methods of independent learning? Clearly, professional reflection on the lives and learning of their students is the basic stimulus.

> My fundamental goals as an educator are expressed in my living relationships with other persons, as students and pupils . . . I am conscious as a teacher of influencing the lives of others with my own life, of letting a selection of the world affect a person through the medium of my own person. I attempt to ensure that my pupils are aware that the educative process is centrally concerned with their meanings. The meanings they create from their experience of phenomena must help them to interpret and change their world of the present and the future. This educative process starts with the pupils' reality, the creation of an atmosphere for learning, and the organisation of Independent Learning Resources.[13]

What are the intentions of the teachers involved in independent learning in science? What kind of scene are they attempting to create in the laboratory?

> 'For our part as science teachers, we must learn to provide learning opportunities differentiated according to the needs of our students, and the students for their part will provide a considerable spectrum of response depending on their age, ability and aptitude.'[14]

> 'Most teachers would admit that an ideal teaching situation is one which permits each child to be treated as an individual in which he is able to progress at his own pace, and in which his mistakes and misconceptions are recognised and clarified immediately, before the next stage in the learning process is embarked upon.'[15]

> 'It is an active sort of learning, offering more initiative and responsibility to the pupil.'[16]

> 'The independent study programme is based on a belief and a hope; the belief that existing school organisational structures and teaching patterns inhibit the full exercise of students' potential for learning, and the hope that a modification can be devised that makes students' experience in learning how to learn whatever they need to learn, the activity of prime importance.'[17]

> 'We feel that by encouraging students to explore ideas and processes when they ask questions about them, we are helping them to learn in the most effective way.'[18]

The above quotations are a fairly representative selection of the expressed intentions of members of the ILIS organisation: science teachers directly involved in school-based curriculum development. It is necessary now to examine in some detail the structure of this organisation, which, in part, they have created to assist the realisation of their intentions and to which they continue to subscribe.

The structure of the ILIS organisation

The development of independent learning in science implies originality on the part of both teachers and students and hence many local variations in both curriculum content and methods of working. From the beginning, it was realised that the essential work of the organisation is local initiative and development, and that such superstructure as it was decided to erect must serve the needs of local groups of teachers, at the same time being very active in stimulating the setting up of new such groups. It was said, before the organisation was established, that 'By placing the main emphasis on the local teams of science teachers, the work is much more likely to be relevant to the needs and purposes of the teachers and students involved.'[19] Such emphasis amounted to a complete reversal of previous structuring of curriculum change. The local teachers now became the writers and originators and it was the responsibility of the central organisation to facilitate their work and to disseminate their achievements.

> A small national organisation would be needed to co-ordinate the work of these regional groups and to assist with the raising of finance, contacting commercial interests, arranging publication of materials, providing feedback to the local and regional groups . . . and generally to maintain oversight of the total project.[20]

Apart from this emphasis on local curriculum development, which derived from the nature of the work to be undertaken, there was a strong and explicit intention, on the part of the founders, to maximise the participation and democratic control of the members of the organisation. These are the primary factors which have determined the structure of the ILIS organisation, and, it is believed, have maintained its vitality and effectiveness.

The central co-ordinating organisation is responsible for the dissemination of information about relevant work in independent learning in science, the establishment and development of contacts between interested teachers, advisers, inspectors, commercial and industrial interests, and publishers, as well as for taking the initiative in extending the work of ILIS through exhibitions and conferences, negotiating grants to the organisation, and also by visiting individuals and small groups of science teachers, with the intention of enabling them to set up local workshop/

resource centres. Most of this work is the responsibility of the Secretary (originally described as the Co-ordinator), but the other officers of the organisation play a considerable part in the process.

The importance of the work of the central organisation has been recognised by Leicestershire Education Committee and the Schools Council. Immediately following the establishment of the organisation, Leicestershire Education Committee provided the Secretary with part-time secretarial assistance for the first two years, also providing him with secondment for the year 1975–6 to assist in the extension of the work for the organisation. The Schools Council granted the ILIS organisation £5,900 for the year 1975–6 to provide for the part-time secondment of three teachers, further secretarial assistance, and general financial support to enable the organisation to continue its work. Since that time the organisation has been self-supporting, its income being derived from members' subscriptions.

The President, Chairman, Secretary, Treasurer and *Newsletter* Editor function as an executive taking decisions based on policy established by the Members General Meeting. The Members General Meeting is the only policy-making body in the organisation. It has, from the beginning, been an open meeting in which any member may participate. It meets once a year at the ASE Annual Meeting. The intention, in making this an open meeting, is to make it possible for the organisation to be controlled by those who are at the grass-roots, the science teachers in the schools. The work of the officers of the organisation is supplemented by the following publications:

The *Newsletter* This publication has now become an important journal of independent learning in science. It is published three times each year. It is intended primarily for communication between members, but copies are sent to teachers and others expressing an interest in the work of the organisation.

The *Directory* This document is supplied to members only and gives details of all the different aspects of independent learning in science at present being undertaken by members. It enables teachers to make contact with others doing the same work as themselves, hopefully leading to the establishment of local workshop/resource centres. This document is prepared by the Secretary and up-dated annually.

The *Catalogue* This, also, is supplied only to members and gives details of independent learning materials currently available from other members. It is up-dated annually.

ILIS *Prospectus* This is a descriptive leaflet outlining the purposes of the organisation and giving details of its structure.

From the start, the members of the ILIS organisation have sought to establish workshop/resource centres to provide:

(i) a meeting ground, often in one school, so that discussion, preparation and evaluation of methods and materials can be properly and firmly established.

(ii) a resource bank of materials for independent learning, together with facilities for copying the materials which the teachers consider are pertinent to their work in the classroom/laboratory.

(iii) a workshop for the development of new resources, relevant to the local needs of teachers.

(iv) a suitable staff for this work to be co-ordinated and developed. The kind and degree of staff employment in these centres is clearly dependent on the extent of support from LEAs and other funding agencies.

The workshop/resource centres are autonomous in all aspects of decision-making, but are encouraged by the central organisation to make their experience and resources available to other similar centres.

With all the enthusiasm in the world, there is clearly little that such centres can achieve unless they are actively supported by the Local Education Authority. For example, teachers are convinced that new kinds of printed materials are essential, and consequently see the provision of reprographic facilities as vitally important, preferably those that can provide them with high-quality printed materials. ILIS has recognised, from the beginning, that such provision may not always be possible for individual schools, and has suggested the sharing of a centre by several local schools, and by groups concerned with more than one area of the curriculum. Provision of reprographic and other facilities is frequently minimal but there are centres, for example the ILEA centre for the Advanced Physics Project for Independent Learning, where at one point in its development there were 'some three Advisory Teachers seconded to it with five ancillary helpers including graphic artists, designers, technicians and clerical assistance'.[21] Obviously the quality of the product used in the laboratory bears a direct relation to this kind of provision. Many teachers would of course go further and consider that the local provision of audio-visual facilities and expertise is essential to the proper development of their schemes for independent learning. ILIS always stressed the importance of maximum local co-operation and has recommended: 'With the assistance, if possible, of the science adviser, local HMI, Warden of the Teachers' Centre, and science staff of the local training establishment, call a meeting of local science teachers to establish whether a local need or opportunity does exist',[22] with the suggestion that 'it will also be important to make maximum use of underused or neglected resources',[23] so avoiding white elephants and unnecessary duplication of effort and resources.

Perhaps the most important consideration from the point of view of the teachers involved in this kind of curriculum development is the extent of teacher secondment. If the job is worth doing at all, and many authorities consider it is, then surely it is worth doing well, and that

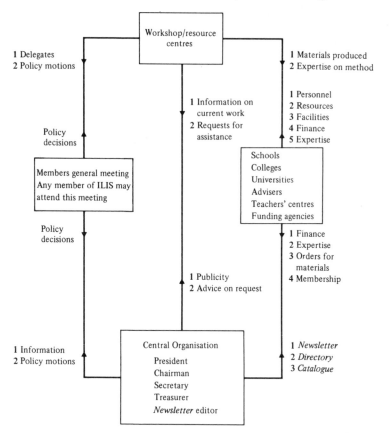

Figure 1.1 *The structure of the ILIS organisation*

means reasonable teacher time being available to local groups.

What I have learned from the workshop, and what I have tried to pass on . . . is that producing individualised learning material is a difficult, painful, time consuming but (if you are patient) rewarding occupation. It is really too much for small groups to tackle on their own, if the members are also teaching full time.

We need many, many workshops with teachers in them who have reduced teaching loads, so that they can devote time to the job. This ought to be easy to arrange when there are too many trained teachers for the Country's needs, and many of them are on the dole. We need to be able to tap the support, already offered, of publishers and industry. (How can we do this more effectively than ILIS has managed so far?)[24]

ILIS and curriculum change

Prior to the establishment of the ILIS organisation in the United Kingdom, there existed a number of examples, notably of individuals, of the operation, in schools and other institutions, of schemes of independent learning in science.[25] These schemes were reported in the literature of science education, from time to time, but there was no attempt made to develop any kind of co-ordination between these various enterprises. The formation of the ILIS organisation, it is suggested, provided that necessary co-ordination which stimulated a greater teacher interest in independent learning, inspired many to become actually involved in its development, and improved professional practice. The arrival of the ILIS organisation provided a focal point, the necessary springboard for the markedly increased activity in this area of curriculum change. In some cases[26] these developments are directly linked to the ILIS organisation while others[27] are less directly connected, but have, nevertheless, in most cases, been staffed in part by ILIS members. These individuals and groups, autonomous as they are, have informed, and been informed by, the ILIS organisation.

What then of the outcomes of this ILIS strategy for curriculum change? Many groups and individuals have emerged since the ILIS organisation was established, producing radical and detailed schemes of independent learning in science, so much so that it is impossible here to give more than the briefest glimpse at what they have achieved, but sufficient, it is hoped, to reveal the interactive components that make the ILIS strategy such an interesting example of school-based curriculum development.

Developments by workshop groups

APPIL – Advanced Physics Project for Independent Learning

This group was established following a consultative meeting consisting of a representative of the ILEA inspectorate, a member of the Open University staff, a representative of the ILIS central organisation and members of the Chelsea College staff, the meeting being convened by the Principal of the Chelsea College. Three important decisions were taken at that initial meeting; first, that there would be the maximum possible teacher involvement; second, that there would be a trial run on one unit of work; third, that the final product would be commercial.

The reasons why we have turned to Independent Learning are important – they arose out of necessity rather than conviction ... to deal with the dual problems which we have with our Science sixths – lack of suitably qualified teachers and small classes.[28]

The group soon realised that a wide diversity of approaches was required in the development of their resources for teaching/learning, and rapidly established high-quality learning sheets, experiment sheets, audio-visual material, computer simulation, discussions, demonstrations, student guides, teacher guides and so on. The entire work has now been published.[29] A detailed evaluation of APPIL[30] has continued during the process of development. The evaluation has been illuminative in the style of Parlett and Hamilton, and not comparative with other styles of teaching, thereby making its own important contribution to the development of the project.

The Evaluation, which aimed to study the impact and effect of APPIL on the classroom situation, has demonstrated once more that curriculum development means teacher development, that the teacher has a vital role to play in the classroom where independent learning material is used. . . .'[31]

BIRD – Biology Independent Resource Development

The organisation of the workshop was based on the realisation, by a group of biology teachers, that to achieve their purposes in developing independent learning methods and resources, a co-operative was essential, the kind of preparation required being unattainable by any one teacher.

The aim is therefore to gather together Biologists who are interested in producing learning situations, using a variety of media and levels of difficulty . . . The overall content of the material would be sufficiently wide to accommodate most G.C.E. and C.S.E. Biology courses.[32]

Teachers meet to discuss the content of each unit of study, making decisions about kinds of activity, use of various kinds of media and so on, these decisions then being subject to checking by the editorial panel. The Art and English departments are involved in the design and language of the resources, as shown in the flow-chart.[33]

CAMOL – Computer Assisted Management Of Learning in Physics

The National Development Programme in Computer Assisted Learning, established at the Education Centre, New University of Ulster, is a development project in the Computer Assisted Management of Learning

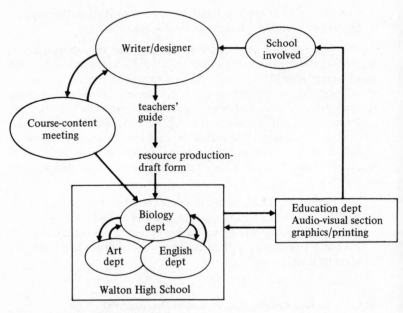

Figure 1.2 *The BIRD workshop*

in Secondary and Tertiary Education. As one element in the project, the Physics Department of the Methodist College, Belfast, has been introducing a system of computer assisted management of their A-level Physics course during the period 1975-9. The material developed at Methodist College, Belfast, is being revised for use in schools within the Birmingham Education Authority. The project grew out of increasing dissatisfaction with conventional methods of teaching A-level Physics:

  (i) The emphasis was on the teaching role of the teacher rather than the learning role of the student. . . .

 (ii) This bias towards 'spoon-feeding' meant that pupils left school unprepared to be students at university where direct supervision of their learning was much less intense. . . .

(iii) Teachers aimed their lessons at the middle third of the class with the result that the more able third who picked up the material first time were bored by the necessary repetition, and the less able third were unable to grasp the new ideas as there was not time to explain the material fully enough for them to understand it.

 (iv) Lessons failed to take into account variation in learning style. . . .

  (v) As the complete course had to be covered in class there was little time for enrichment material.[34]

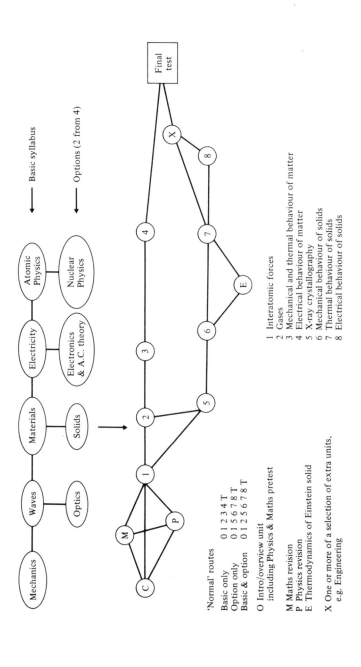

Mechanics — Waves — Materials — Electricity — Atomic Physics

Optics, Solids, Electronics & A.C. theory, Nuclear Physics

Basic syllabus →

Options (2 from 4) →

'Normal' routes

Basic only   0 1 2 3 4 T
Option only   0 1 5 6 7 8 T
Basic & option 0 1 2 5 6 7 8 T

O Intro/overview unit
  including Physics & Maths pretest

M Maths revision
P Physics revision
E Thermodynamics of Einstein solid

X One or more of a selection of extra units,
  e.g. Engineering

1 Interatomic forces
2 Gases
3 Mechanical and thermal behaviour of matter
4 Electrical behaviour of matter
5 X-ray crystallography
6 Mechanical behaviour of solids
7 Thermal behaviour of solids
8 Electrical behaviour of solids

Figure 1.3 *CAMOL flow diagram*

Out of this dissatisfaction there grew a very extensive and well-planned development of independent learning allied with the use of the computer as an aid to the management of the learning process, rather than as a teaching machine.

Students work at their own rates on individual modules of study with reading matter, problems, practical work, audio-visual materials and tests. Each module is designed to be covered in 1–2 weeks and includes some or all of the following –

(i) Introduction including references to syllabuses and textbooks, and information on the relation of the module to other modules, other subjects and the outside world.
(ii) Prerequisite knowledge – including mathematics.
(iii) Pre-test to assess prerequisite knowledge.
(iv) Answers to pre-test, and comments.
(v) Remedial material, if required.
(vi) A list of objectives to let students know what they should have learned by the end of the module.
(vii) Main material organised into sections which may be experimental, reading, answering questions or using audio-visual material.
(viii) Post-test to see if objectives have been achieved.
(ix) Optional sections for those who have covered the main material.
(x) Summary for revision.
(ix) Notes for teachers.[35]

a computer marks each question in a multiple choice test at the end of a two week unit of study, then gives corrective comments on the wrong answers turning the test into a learning situation. On the basis of the overall results of the test, and other information, the student is routed to a choice of succeeding units, or to remedial material, or to see his teacher.[36]

Clowne School science scheme[37]

This scheme, concerned with work in the early years of the secondary school, places its emphasis on small-group work with students, rather than in the development of resources suitable for an individualised approach, at the same time recognising that 'If the above ideas are taken to the extreme, an individualised learning situation might be advocated'. The motivation that pushed the three teachers responsible into devising the scheme, was based on 'an increasing concern on the part of the science staff over what was being taught and the method used'. From this concern eventually crystallised the following areas of dissatisfaction:

(a) Pupils were not being put into situations where they had to think sufficiently about the problem under investigation.

(b) The scientific method was not being taught effectively.

(c) Manipulative skills and practical techniques were not being sufficiently developed for the demands of upper school science.

(d) Remedial pupils . . . were being taught as a separate class and there was a tendency to expect too little of them, whereas in fact some were just as able in science as pupils in higher streams.

(e) Even when classes were streamed the ability range was still quite large making the same approach inappropriate for all pupils.

(f) Because of wide differences in pre-secondary school experience, some of the work being taught had been covered by some but not all pupils. This makes it difficult to interest all pupils in the same investigation at the same time, and in any case is it reasonable to expect all pupils to have the same interest at the same time?

(g) Insufficient attention could be given to original ideas presented by the pupils.

(h) The enthusiasm shown by the first-year pupils was not being sustained.

(i) There was insufficient communication and flow of ideas between teachers involved with the same work and between teachers and pupils.

From the point of view of the teachers concerned, three important features of the scheme were recognised: their ability to adapt to a new situation; good relationships within the team; opportunity for frequent meetings. Further developments[38] are being made by this team who meanwhile 'deplore the situation whereby through lack of available time, the necessary research work is not done through collaboration with practising teachers but too often by persons in institutions removed from the actual practice of teaching school-aged children.'

GLOSILIS – Gloucestershire ILIS workshop group[39]

Members of this group of teachers had considered the matter of independent learning for some time before they finally felt ready to produce ILIS materials for years one and two: 'it took time for sufficient of us to be convinced that we really needed some other way of coping with mixed ability groups and that ILIS was worth a try.' Apparently conviction came as a result of looking at the schemes in operation at two Hertfordshire schools, Knights Templar at Baldock and Sir James Altham at South Oxley, through the eyes of two teachers already well experienced in methods of independent learning. The outcome was the formation of three writing groups.

Actually what goes on at their meetings — they meet every two or three weeks — is the shredding of each other's efforts which have been written or rewritten since the last meeting. Of course, working in separate groups we have to have some co-ordination and common policy.

An important basis for their common policy was a document they described as 'Appendix A' as shown below.

Appendix A
Independent Learning In Science
Gloucestershire Groups

Centre	Chairman
Cinderford TC	D R Hall — Whitecross School
Gloucestershire TC	R Hawkey — The Archway School
Science Centre	J A Payne — Churchdown School
	G S Todd — Stroud Girls High School

1 The task of each group is to write independent learning material for use in years 1 and 2 of Secondary Schools and based on the Nuffield Combined Science (11-13) Project materials.

2 (a) Before beginning to write a contribution, a Group must decide and state the objectives of the learning with special reference to:
    (i) acquisition of basic scientific vocabulary
    (ii) the skill(s) which pupils should acquire
    (iii) the concepts they should grasp
    These will be stated in the Teachers' Guide.

  (b) It will be necessary to state the pupils' previous learning (in terms of the Combined Science Materials) which the worksheet(s) assume. This, too, will be stated in the Teachers' Guide.

3 Guidance on the presentation of work:
  (a) Directions for experimental work should be given in as pictorial a fashion as possible.
  (b) Where pupils' writing or response is required in their notebooks, the work is to be marked at either side by double lines.
  (c) Care should be taken in providing for pupils' responses to the immediate observations and/or immediate outcomes of an experiment to make them as simple and unequivocal (objective) as possible.
  (d) As far as practicable, questions prompting these immediate responses should be interlarded with the experimental directions.

(e) Subsequently, the questions should become increasingly open-ended.

(f) Where appropriate, back-up and extension work should be provided.

4 The principal activity at local Group meetings will be the 'shreding' of members' drafts.

5 Material redrafted after shredding should be sent to the Science Centre for photocopying and distribution for trials.

6 Comments for feedback from trials should be written on a copy of the worksheet to which alteration and amendment can also be made. (See Appendix B.)

7 The originating Group will be responsible for co-ordinating feedback on its material. The final amended versions will again be photocopied and distributed by the Science Centre.

8 Final versions shall be produced in as attractive a style and format as economically possible.

9 There will be at least two plenary meetings each year for general business, co-ordination and feedback from trials.

Apart from the regular meetings for production and evaluation of materials, based on this policy, the group also organised day conferences for the purpose of forward planning where they dealt with such matters as 'how the feedback should be recorded', and 'how pupil assessment can be carried out'. They also considered it important in these conferences to 'feed in people's experience of how things have been going in schools so that we can learn from each other's successes and mistakes'. Their conclusion was that 'By getting away from the usual cottage industry of schools each doing their own thing, we are not only getting our material faster, we are learning from each other in the process and the quality of the material has improved greatly'.

There are many other examples of developments by local workshop groups,[40] but perhaps the above are sufficient to demonstrate the extent of common intentions and strategies. The ILIS organisation has never played a direct role, for such was never its aim, in the development of these workshop groups, but it has acted, it is suggested, as an important inspirational and informative focal point, without which the secure foundation of much of this school-based curriculum development would never have been realised.

Developments by individual teachers

Both before and since the formation of the ILIS organisation, much of the work of establishing independent learning in science in schools has been informed and sustained by the pioneering work of individual teachers. Indeed it is most unlikely that the organisation would have been established at all, or survived, but for the work of these individuals.[41] Although perhaps of subsidiary importance, it also ought to be said that the recognition, by various educational journals and publishers,[42] of the importance of the work of individual teachers, served to establish connections between these teachers, which provided the basis for the discussions which finally led to the formation of ILIS.

The innovative work of individual science teachers in the development of independent learning in schools has been fully described elsewhere,[43] and it is only possible here to give the briefest indication of what has been achieved. Through a perusal of the references it will be apparent that those achievements are very extensive and are firmly based on long and thoughtful experience with students in the laboratory. What will also be apparent is the importance of the mutual interaction of these teachers both at local and national level, providing further stimulus for their work and the improvement of it. In general terms, then, what have they achieved?

First, they have firmly established their credibility and that of independent learning in science as a real and viable alternative to the methods of traditional class teaching. Extensive reporting in the literature of science education; openness, in allowing visits by fellow teachers to see students at work; the quality of the work achieved with students; the integrity and thoroughness of the innovators themselves: all these factors have made their contribution to the realisation that independent learning is now an accepted, relevant and firmly based practice in the methodology of science education.

Second, they have contributed a great deal, in the exploration and elaboration of the principles and practice of independent learning, to a fuller understanding of its potential. Early innovations suggest new ideas which trigger off new developments — an essential process in the improvement of practice.

> My discussions in the group I attended led me to examine my attitudes to the written materials I have produced and use . . . it may well be possible, and desirable, to operate independent learning situations with less reliance on the structured worksheets. This year I am exploring ways of doing this. . . .[44]

Third, they have produced the necessary resources for independent learning across the total science curriculum, especially for those parts represented by modern syllabuses. Reference to the ILIS *Directory* reveals the considerable extent of this interest and development. The ILIS *Catalogue* gives details of the resources which are available to other teachers. Many, many teachers have used these resources, either as they stand, or modified to suit local requirements, so saving themselves considerable time in development work. The national and local co-operative emphasis in curriculum development could and should be extensively developed within science education, and perhaps into other areas of the curriculum.

ILIS: an evaluation?[45]

So far, only a few evaluative studies of the work of ILIS and its members[46] have been completed, and it is clear that the bulk of such work still remains to be done. ILIS has, for some time, pressed the urgency of such studies, believing, in these days of a major shift to independent learning in schools, that they will play an important role in the improvement of the quality of that learning: 'the time is coming when more objective research and evaluation should be devoted to establishing the effectiveness of independent learning, and so prepare the way for further innovations.'[47]

The intention, here, is further to encourage the dialogue, to pose some of the problems raised by certain kinds of evaluation, to argue some of the possible solutions, so that some meaningful strategy for evaluation might be evolved. At the same time, it is important to consider the below-the-surface, ongoing evaluation by teachers, which, it is suggested, is fuelling the ever increasing use of independent learning in science.

'A major change in teaching methods has been towards catering for children as individuals rather than a large group or class.'[48] The teachers in ILIS today share, with the originators of this organisation, the gut feeling that independent learning is right — right for them, right for their students. They share a similar philosophy of education, and, within it, they are developing their own perspective on independent learning in response to the local situation they know, and with which they are intimately involved. At local and national level a continuing process of evaluation goes on, more and more teachers committing themselves and their students to independent learning, apparently convinced that they have made a proper evaluation before taking that step. The continuing emergence of schemes of independent learning in science is, no doubt, in part based on a considered evaluation of the work that has been documented over the years, but the final decision, it is thought, is much more likely to be traceable to what can perhaps be called 'gut evaluation' — an inner perception that it makes sense; consistency with fundamental educational aims; a stirring of the imagination; that conglomeration of sentiments and values, never quite sorted out, but which nevertheless informs and determines many of life's major decisions. Can we supplement this evaluation with other kinds which will encourage greater confidence in and understanding of what is being attempted? It seems we must. Despite the documented evidence and the continued growth of independent learning in science, gut evaluation is not adequate for the decision-makers — or is it? In their rejection of the ILIS 'Proposal for a five-year support programme for independent learning in science',[49] by the Science Committee of the Schools Council, much play was made, despite the known inherent difficulties and the lack of suitable funds in the ILIS organisation, of the need for objective evaluation, whatever that might mean or achieve. What was the basis of their evaluation of ILIS? Was it not the very same gut evaluation that they implied should be ignored? There is the suspicion that evaluation for decision-makers is a myth, rarely considered, decision-making being much more concerned with struggle for power, and far less than some will admit with objective study. If rational evaluation plays so small a part in the upper reaches of educational decision-making, then why the insistence on imposing it on the teacher in the classroom? Certainly, whatever the possible limitations of leaving the evaluation to teachers, all must recognise that it is their gut evaluation that has determined, and will continue to determine, the kind and degree of curriculum change taking place in schools.

The central problem in our evaluation of ILIS, 'our' meaning science teachers, HMI, science advisers, members of Schools Council Science Committee and other decision-makers, as well as students, parents, and not least of all members of ILIS itself, is posed by Harlen.

> Their work has encouraged wider appreciation that to provide children with equal opportunities for learning means giving them different learning activities rather than equal learning experience — in other words, to adapt educational materials to the pupil rather than vice versa. The adaptation has to be programmed into the materials or given into the hands of the teacher. In either case, the consequences for developing and evaluating curriculum materials which purport to cater for individual differences are profound. Evaluation must be concerned not only with the characteristics, variables and processes relating to the class as a whole, but also with individuals, each with his own set of abilities, preferences, styles of learning, attitudes, interests and past experiences. It is a formidable task to take account of all these factors and it requires a change in conception of what are relevant models for gathering and analysing the data.[50]

Hence the heading 'ILIS: an evaluation?' It is difficult to see the way ahead, decision-makers on the one hand demanding objective evaluation, professional evaluators stressing the formidable nature of such a task, convinced teachers frustrated by the decision-makers. There is no intention here of attempting to achieve what the professional evaluators find very difficult, but, until the professionals can produce something better, the following suggestions are offered:

1 Recognise, that it is very doubtful, that before making any new move in their work, teachers read, even if they know of them, any appropriate studies. A few might — most of them form their own gut evaluation, based on their previous experience, discussion with other teachers in their local groups and schools, the personal prejudices of their own education and professional training, and, of course and quite rightly, in the light of local facilities available in terms of resources and time. That evaluation is, that what ILIS is doing is right and meaningful for them and their students. It is that evaluation which is their driving force — their dynamic for change — and it is creating a new vision of what science education can be. Essentially the teachers are asking the decision-makers to trust that evaluation.

2 Assistance is needed for the establishment of more school-based evaluation studies exemplified by the Schools Council's project *Improving learning for 11 to 14 year olds in mixed ability science groups.*[51]

This will be a co-operative activity between learners, teachers, lecturers, scientists and industrialists. The teachers will express their intentions verbally, in writing and with practical examples. The learners will be interviewed and video-taped whilst working to detect the state of their scientific activity. The view will be taken that language is inadequate to express a person engaged in scientific activity, it is the kind of phenomenon that can only be shown. The evaluation sessions will be dialogues between the above people as they attempt to make available to each other their interpretations of the teachers' intentions and the learners' activities, and the assumptions on which they are based. Records will include written statements, transcripts of interviews and evaluation sessions and video-tapes of the learners' activities.

When teachers have reached this point in their evaluation, then they are more likely to feel receptive to the professional evaluator's experimental methods of data-gathering, testing hypotheses, and building up a communication network for consultancy and the circulation of case studies.

In conclusion

The desirability of individualising instruction is no longer questioned by anyone. The objections to it are concerned chiefly with the application of the theory to classroom conditions. Among the partial solutions offered to the problem is that of differentiated requirements, or the practice of varying the amount of work to be accomplished in accordance with the ability of the individual pupils of a group.

Or to quote another expert in the same publication,

> Under the old regime, in the effort to give different children the same subject matter in the same length of time, the quality of the children's work, the degree of their mastery, varied from poor to excellent, as attested by their report cards. But under the new technique of individual education, instead of quality varying, time varies; a child may take as much time as he needs to master a unit of work, but master it he must. The common essentials, by definition, are those knowledges and skills needed by everyone. To allow many children, therefore, to pass through school with hazy and inadequate grasp of them, as one must under the class lock-step scheme, is to fail in one of the functions of the school.

One could be forgiven for thinking that these were quotations from current educational literature, but they are in fact statements made over fifty years ago by Reavis of the University of Chicago High School and Washbourne of the Winnetka Public Schools in the 1925 yearbook of the National Society for the Study of Education entitled, *Adapting the Schools to Individual Differences.*

One could spend a long time, and probably a great deal of wasted effort, probing the reasons as to why, during the span of half a century, so little implementation of ideas regarding independent learning has taken place. It might be suggested that much of the inertia might be traceable to limitations in technology, expertise, and the necessary experimentation, or possibly the conservatism of teachers themselves, or indeed, an interest by the controlling powers in education, local authorities, training establishments, the inspectorate, publishers and other commercial interests in maintaining the status quo. Wherever one might place the blame there is now no doubt, following the emergence of the mixed-ability group, that all these areas are undergoing a shake-up in their thinking and practice. This shake-up has brought in its wake cries of anguish and a fear for the future of education in our schools. Such a reaction is to be expected, and although, it is believed, not really justified, might have many positive and useful consequences in practice. Reasoned scepticism is an important base for any valid development in education, and it is good that the dialogue has been joined, and that the cut and thrust of argument and counter argument goes on apace, but it is also important that from that base should arise a determination to see that the development of this alternative in education is given the power for effective promotion. It is right and essential that questions should be asked, that local experiments should first take place, but once the evidence is there, once the affirmation has been given, then the power to make the necessary changes must be made available. Mixed-ability groups are here to stay (have they not always been with us?), but, by and large, teachers are being left to get on with solving their problems and preparing their schemes, in the best way they know. Some of the work being done is outstanding and is making a marked contribution to the further improvement of independent learning – but a pat on the back is not good enough. If what is being done is good and valid, then a firm commitment of the necessary resources is essential if it is to be done well, and if it is to be the pattern of development for the next fifty years. Today we do have the technology, the expertise and a considerable amount of experience, but what we lack – not for the first time – is a firm endeavour in our educational establishment, to take a sure grip on what has been started and to follow it through. To educate according to the age, ability and aptitude of the individual child has long been our aim. We are now on the brink of giving that most laudable aim real life and meaning, but there is a danger that through lack of vision we shall fail even to give it breath.

The shake-up in our educational thinking and strategy that the adoption of mixed-ability grouping has brought and implies will and should go on, but it would be nothing but meaningless aggravation unless there was also the shake-out. The adoption of mixed-ability groups needs no defence, if only because it has already served one great purpose, that is, to force us back to our beginnings, the education of the individual, and the consequent establishment of a better and more natural relationship with that individual. On that basis we have begun a new synthesis, weaving together the many important strands from the past, at the same time using our imagination in forging new patterns, new ideas, new visions: that must be the shake-out. The place that we begin to pick up the threads of this synthesis is with those who have initiated the necessary changes the imaginative and adventurous teachers, not inhibited by the difficulties, not blinded by negative pedagogy from certain quarters, but alive to the opportunities and bringing their ideas to fruition.

Three central policies characterise the work of the unit: the first based on the principle of intensive support; the second on the principle of continuous teacher involvement; third on an evolutionary view of educational change . . . Throughout, the approach must be to recognise the possibility of radical transformations of the assumptions and concepts within which schools operate. Teachers need the opportunites to experience the practical alternatives, to make their own choices and thus to become personally involved in the history of these ideas.[52]

That brings us back to where this study of the ILIS model of school-based curriculum development began, with the teachers in the schools; but finally, perhaps, we ought to consider the possibility of one new and important development in our co-operative model of curriculum change: a national centre. Detailed discussion and consideration, by those currently involved in independent learning, would need to be given to this idea, so that such a centre did satisfy a real and not an imaginary need. Such a centre would play a major role in the setting up of new workshop/resource centres, arranging secondment of teachers, making some direct contribution to the training of teachers, providing a platform for national conferences, and generally bringing the developments in independent learning to the attention of all those engaged in the business of education. Such a centre might also be engaged in a wide range of studies in assessment and evaluation techniques, in co-operation with the workshop/resource centres, a contribution, which has long been sought, to the achievement of better understanding of and standards in the work that has so far been done.

> ILIS must continue to help, wherever it can, to give support to the providers of in-service and initial training. Above all, it must give teachers confidence in what they are doing . . . it must let them know that they are not alone in using independent learning as one of the methods of teaching science.[53]

Notes

1 Examination of the ILIS membership in the *Directory* indicates teachers from grammar, public, secondary modern, comprehensive schools and sixth-form colleges.
2 For example, D. J. Reid and P. Booth, 'The use of individual learning with the Nuffield biology course', *School Science Review,* vol. 50, 493, 1969; and E. L. Green, 'Individualised learning in physics', *School Science Review,* vol. 54, 260, 1972.
3 For example, D. P. Bosworth, 'Teaching science individually through programmes', *School Science Review,* vol. 48, 702, 1967; and M. D. Wilson, 'Programmed learning in biology', *School Science Review,* vol. 49, 689, 1968.
4 E. L. Green, 'A new deal in science', *Times Educational Supplement,* 6 April 1973.
5 E. L. Green, 'Individual and small group methods in the teaching of science', report on the conference held at Countesthorpe College, 17–19 April 1973, published by ILIS.
6 The *Newsletter* is published three times a year. The *Directory* and *Catalogue* are revised annually.

7   E. L. Green (ed.), *Towards Independent Learning in Science*, London, Hart-Davis Educational, 1976, p. 166.
8   *Schools Council Working Paper*, no. 10, paragraph 1.
9   Ibid., paragraphs 6, 7 and 11.
10 Ibid., paragraphs 16, 17 and 18.
11 Ibid., paragraph 16.
12 Ibid., paragraph 17.
13 J. Whitehead, in ILIS *Newsletter*, no. 4, October 1974, p. 1.
14 E. L. Green (ed.), *Towards Independent Learning in Science*, p. 3.
15 M. D. Wilson, 'Programmed learning in biology'.
16 D. Foster, 'Resources for learning development unit', ILIS *Newsletter*, no. 9, June 1976.
17 J. V. De Rose, 'Independent study in high school chemistry: a progress report', *Chemical Education*, vol. 47, 553, 1970.
18 J. Shapland and P. Watson, 'Beyond the worksheet', ILIS *Newsletter*, January 1977, p. 4.
19 E. L. Green, 'A new deal in science'.
20 Ibid.
21 J. Lewis, 'Independent learning in science in London', ILIS *Newsletter*, no. 5, February 1975.
22 E. L. Green, 'Co-ordinator's column', ILIS *Newsletter*, no. 9, June 1976.
23 Ibid.
24 J. Temple, 'How to set up an ILIS workshop, and how not to', ILIS *Newsletter*, no. 7, October 1975.
25 See examples in E. L. Green (ed.), *Towards Independent Learning in Science*.
26 P. Herbert, Elliott School, ILEA, for the 'Quest' project; P. Homan-Berry, Salisbury workshop; P. Ashworth, Cornwall workshop.
27 D. J. McCullough, workshop on Medium Term Independent Learning in Physics for N. Ireland GCE O-level syllabus; M. Brown, CAMOL project, Methodist College, Belfast; J. Whitehead, workshop, 'Improving learning for 11–14 year olds in mixed ability science groups'.
28 J. Lewis, 'Independent learning in science in London'.
29 In 1979 by John Murray.
30 G. M. de Gonzales and J. Gilbert, 'APPIL: Some general aspects of its evaluation', ILIS *Newsletter*, no. 15, November 1978.
31 Ibid.
32 B. Nicholas, 'Biology Independent Resource Development', ILIS *Newsletter*, no. 15, November 1978.
33 Ibid.
34 M. Brown, 'Computer assisted management of learning in physics at Methodist College, Belfast', ILIS *Newsletter*, no. 8, February 1976.
35 Ibid.
36 Ibid.
37 I. J. Burden, A. K. Turner and M. J. Whittaker, 'Clowne Science Scheme — a method based course for the early years in secondary schools', *School Science Review*, vol. 57, 7, 1975.

38 I. J. Burden, J. B. Howe and M. J. Whittaker, 'A problem solving approach to science teaching in the 11–13 year age', ILIS *Newsletter,* no. 13, December 1977.
39 N. Steers, 'G.L.O.S.I.L.I.S.', ILIS *Newsletter,* no. 10, October 1976.
40 'ILEA 11–13 Project', ILIS *Newsletter,* no. 11, March 1977 (no author given). M. Brown and D. J. McCullogh, 'Medium term independent learning in physics', ILIS *Newsletter,* no. 4, October 1974; no. 5, February 1975; no. 8, February 1976 and no. 10, October 1976. P. Herbert, 'Quest', ILIS *Newsletter,* no. 6, June 1975. A. Grant and P. Homan-Berry, 'Salisbury Workshop', ILIS *Newsletter,* no. 8, February 1976; no. 9, June 1976; and no. 10, October 1976. D. Foster, 'Resources for Learning Development Unit', ILIS *Newsletter,* no. 5, February 1975; no. 9, June 1976; no. 11, March 1977, and no. 14, April 1978.
41 E. L. Green (ed.), *Towards Independent Learning in Science.*
42 *School Science Review, Physics Education, Education in Chemistry, Journal of Biological Education, Times Educational Supplement.*
43 See ILIS *Newsletters.*
44 J. Shapland, 'Do worksheets work', ILIS *Newsletter,* no. 4, October 1974.
45 Based on E. L. Green, 'ILIS . . . An Evaluation', paper presented to the Evaluators' Group of the Schools Council on 19 November 1976.
46 J. Whitehead, 'Improving learning for 11 to 14 year olds in mixed ability science groups', Wiltshire Curriculum Development Centre, 1976: G. M. de Gonzales and J. Gilbert, 'APPIL: some general aspects of its evaluation', ILIS *Newsletter,* no. 15, November 1978.
47 E. L. Green (ed.), *Towards Independent Learning in Science,* p. 36.
48 W. Harlen, 1976, 'Schools Council Research Studies', in D. Tawney (ed.), *Curriculum Evaluation Today, Trends and Implications,* Macmillan Education.
49 A Round 1 Proposal to Schools Council, November 1976.
50 W. Harlen, 'Schools Council Research Studies'.
51 J. Whitehead, published by the Wiltshire Curriculum Development Centre, Swindon.
52 P. Waterhouse, 'How resourceful can you get', *Times Educational Supplement,* 4 April 1975.
53 M. Frazer, 'Presidential Address', ILIS *Newsletter,* no. 12, July 1977.

Chapter 2

Children Investigating and teachers writing
Ken Wild

This chapter falls into two parts. The first describes the work of teachers in Staffordshire schools in producing a set of booklets to help children involved with Science 5-13 and similar activities. The second part considers the similar work of a wider group of teachers preparing booklets for another national project — the Nuffield Working with Science Project — this time working mainly within rather than largely outside the project itself.

Children Investigating

Children Investigating is a set of booklets devised and written by Staffordshire teachers to provide science-based materials for use mainly with children in the age range 8-13. The booklets are intended as source materials for teachers. Each can be read through in less than an hour. Each contains a flow-chart linking a particular topic to related areas of knowledge, a statement of objectives which could be achieved by a child, starting points and activities designed to explore and develop the theme, and numerous questions intended to stimulate curiosity and give direction and shape to the work.

The booklets are not intended as pupil books. The writers recognised the need for such material but quailed at the prospect of writing for children other than those they *taught*. Their apprehensions were not eased by the publication of the Nuffield Combined Science Continuation Project *Themes for Middle Years*. They regard the study sheets and activity cards of that project as no more than suggestions of what could be among the source material, writing to suit the needs of children in their classes. Generally they would not use the project materials as an essential part of their work in science. For them the appropriate pupil guides have not yet been written. Perhaps the new Schools Council

Learning Through Science project will be considered to be more success-ful. Trials of this project are beginning in Staffordshire and elsewhere in 1979–80 and several of the teachers who worked on Children Investi-gating will be trials teachers on, and possibly contributors to, Learning Through Science.

The idea for a collection of booklets on the theme of children investi-gating stemmed from the work of a group of teachers in primary and in the lower end of secondary schools. In their teaching, these teachers had been drawing on sources such as Nuffield Junior Science, Schools Council Science 5–13, Nuffield Combined Science, Evans Integrated Themes, Scottish Integrated Science and a host of other references. The teachers had been members of, or had contributed to, Local Authority in-service courses and summer schools and had come to the conclusion that there was a real need for some short topic booklets explaining how to introduce, keep going and make use of science-based activities.

The movement, within the authority, towards a three-tier organisation of schools focused attention upon the place of science in the 'middle school'. Much thought, discussion and energy has gone into this issue and the teachers developing Children Investigating contributed to and drew from that debate. Initially the emphasis was upon the science compo-nent of the curriculum in 9–13 middle schools but, following Local Authority reorganisation, the needs of children who go on to high schools at the age of 12 had also to be taken into account.

The questions to be settled included: What is Science? What is its reference to children in the middle years of schooling? Why teach Science? What kind of Science should be taught and at what age? Can we plan an open-ended situation *and* allow for concept development?

Looking for answers to these and similar questions brought the teachers quickly to the heart of one of *the* debates about science in the curriculum — the question whether it is seen as a body of knowledge (the 'content' view) or whether it is a way of looking at things (the 'method' view). This same debate has more recently exercised the Science Working Party of the Assessment of Performance Unit and those search-ing for the science component of the core curriculum. Table 2.1 sum-marises the extreme positions of the two viewpoints.

In real terms these apparently opposing views need not be exclusive or incompatible. However, teachers and schools are more likely to tend towards the 'content' view which is seen to be more relevant to most examinations and teaching syllabuses. The writers of Children Investi-gating had to debate and agree upon where the emphasis should be placed. When the overall picture of the kind of science which is appro-priate to the needs of the children had been decided, the team began to write down the objectives and the kind of subject matter which could sensibly be included. The writers had to decide what sort of things

TABLE 2.1 *The 'content' and 'method' view of science*

Content view	Method view
Science is a body of knowledge	Science is a way of looking at things
Teachers think it important to teach part of that knowledge	Teachers think it important to help children to become adept at using that method
To that end they tell children, explain to children, show children how and verify for them	To that end they question children, stimulate them to think and ask them why
They give the answers to questions and tell children where to find the answers	They help children find out for themselves, they answer a question with a question and help the children to look for the answers
They encourage children to follow 'the book'	They encourage children to have an open mind about 'the book'
They provide the mind with information	They try to get the mind working
The teacher is the *oracle* who prepares work for use with children from the standpoint — what do I want them to know?	The teacher is the *guide* who prepares an environment for the children to work in from the standpoint — how can I stimulate the children to find out what they need to know?

a 13-year-old should have encountered, and to identify the basic knowledge of science appropriate to the 13-year-old from their first-hand experience of which topics are appropriate for the various ages of children.

The Science 5–13 Project was central to the development of teacher expectations and concerns. Trials of the project in Staffordshire played a crucial part in the sequence of events which was to lead to the production of Children Investigating. The project was set up in 1967 and was established to

> consolidate and extend the work on primary science teaching initiated by the Nuffield Junior Science Project, paying particular attention to the needs of older junior pupils, and pupils in the early years of secondary school. The main work of the project has been to identify objectives for guiding pupils' education through science, to relate them to stages in pupils' educational development and to exemplify ways in which these objectives might be achieved. The aim of the

development work has been to assist teachers to help children through discovery methods, to gain experience and understanding of the environment and to develop their powers of thinking effectively about it. (Science 5–13 *Newsletter,* 1970)

Twelve Staffordshire schools were included in those schools in England and Wales which took part in the trials of the materials produced by the Science 5–13 Project. The twelve schools were in three groups of four each with a group leader from one of the schools and with the trials effort co-ordinated by the Science Adviser. The group leaders went on an intensive course organised by the national project team and on their return met at three weekly intervals, along with the Science Adviser, to discuss the development of the project work in the schools. The schools were in close liaison with, and visited by, the national project organiser and his colleagues.

Following the trials, which were conducted along the lines required by the national organisers, a summer school at a local college brought together most of the teachers in the trial schools and a number of others from other schools who were interested, and allowed them to establish extensive contact with each other and with the national team. The three group leaders from the schools played a major part in this summer school. The summer school was followed by still more extensive trials of the project materials on a similar basis in the following year. But at this stage the initiative was being firmly grasped by the teachers in the schools themselves, not only by the group leaders but by a number of others also so that within the trial schools, the material being produced came increasingly to arise from the initiatives of the teachers and the requirements of the schools rather than remaining pre-determined by the teachers' guides produced by the national project team. The earlier formal meetings which took place when the focus of the project was centred on the national team gradually gave way to a series of school-based initiatives in which the teachers, though still working within the broad lines determined by the national project, were evolving a series of distinctive curriculum strategies for teaching science in their schools.

This became still further the case when discussions began concerning the curriculum for middle-school children in the age range 8–13. The need to work out distinctive curricula for these schools, that had previously not existed, became an important and urgent task. The authority allowed these new schools considerable autonomy in making their curricular decisions, and the opportunity to develop appropriate science curricula was taken up fully by the teachers who had initially been drawn together under the banner of the 5–13 project. The detailed programmes of meetings and consultations within the individual schools are, as is characteristic in school-based curriculum development, not available in detail. Some of the most important discussions occur spontaneously and informally in the staff room, in corridors and in the homes of teachers working after normal school hours. Of the intensity of the discussions there is little doubt and the results are clearly to be seen in the Staffordshire primary and middle schools. Some of the more tangible results are also to be seen in the scope and range of the Children Investigating booklets.

The following strategy for writing the booklets was evolved:

1 Select a topic
2 Draw up a flow-chart; refine the flow-chart
3 Think about objectives
4 Anticipate what children might be doing
5 Consider what the Schools Council Science 5–13 Project and the Nuffield Combined Science Teaching Project have to offer. Keep in mind other sources and own ideas
6 List the requirements which could be needed
7 Devise questions for the teacher to bear in mind to stimulate activity to keep the work going and to guide the children towards the objectives.

It was intended that the booklets would be seen as 'on-the-shelf offers' which teachers would adapt and try with their classes.

The complete list of Units is as follows:

Series 1 (printed in 1975)	Series 2 (printed in 1976)	Series 3 (printed in 1977)
Rain	*Acids and Alkalis*	*Air Around Us*
Colour in Plants	*Use of Metals*	*Plant Growth*
Flowers	*Soil*	*Patterns in Nature – Plants*
Rocks	*Canals*	*Cloths and Threads*
Electricity	*Particles*	*Heating and Burning*
Movement	*Streams and Rivers*	*Floating and Sinking*
Measurement	*Sorting and Patterns*	*Oil*
How Life Begins	*Light*	*Patterns in Nature – Animals*
House	*Bird Table*	*Hedgerows*
Sound		*Woodland*
Bridges		
Trees		
Spiders		
Six-Legged Beasties		
Wet and Dry		

A teachers' guide to Children Investigating was produced in 1977.

The booklets have been compiled primarily for the 8–13 age range of pupils, but some are more advanced than others. The grid in Figure 2.1 is an attempt to pinpoint the most appropriate age for their use.

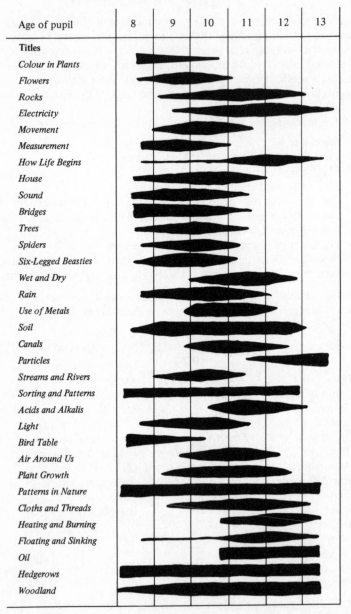

Figure 2.1 *Most appropriate age for use of each Children Investigating unit*

The age used is chronological age, with a pupil of average ability; to have attempted to use the age of mental development would have created extreme difficulties. The age range where an individual booklet can be used is shown by the length of the band, and the maximum thickness indicates the most appropriate age for its use. Obviously, with minor adjustments or modifications of activities, concepts and contents, a teacher could make good use of a booklet with pupils of different ages.

The booklets produced thus far cover a very wide field of scientific study. There has been no attempt to include all aspects of science in any way, but to make available a selection of ideas on fairly major themes. It is not intended to preclude the preparations of further booklets should the need arise, or if teachers are stimulated in this direction, either from their work with children in schools or as a 'spin-off' from future courses.

It is hoped to incorporate any further ideas in the form of a newsletter, on an annual basis, circulated to schools. This newsletter would offer information, modifications and extensions to booklets, and articles of interest relating to their use. Any ideas or items for inclusion in such a newsletter are gratefully welcomed by the Science Advisers who are also happy to visit schools to discuss any problems, difficulties or ideas relating to the Children Investigating series.

Nuffield Working with Science Project

Other Staffordshire teachers were involved with a somewhat similar pattern of events which led to the publication of another national curriculum development project. This project set out to invite groups of teachers to come together and develop science-based materials appropriate to the needs and interests of less academic post-16 students. The Working with Science Project founded by the Nuffield Foundation is of comparatively recent origin and takes into account far more fully than many earlier projects, the important need for initiatives to spring from within the school rather than arriving from outside it. Guided by the experience of projects such as Science 5–13 and Nuffield Combined Science, the project's model from the outset was to work within the schools and groups of teachers were set up with a clear understanding that they would be working collectively yet producing materials with their own schools and their own needs in mind. The workshop groups were formed in Manchester, Staffordshire, Gloucestershire, Leicestershire and Hertfordshire initially. Each began with a three-day writing conference in which the central team of the project explored not curricula but methods of producing materials. In the three years of the project's life, the workshop groups have produced some forty units, tried them out

47

in a number of schools, revised and evaluated them and made them available, through a distribution system established by the central team, to each other and to other schools. Table 2.2 summarises the development of the Working with Science Project.

TABLE 2.2 *Summary of the development of the Working with Science Project*

Year	Activity	Team
1971–2	The need for materials for the new sixth former was established The original project team was formed A working paper was produced and circulated for comment Two sample Units were written	*Organiser* R. A. Finch *Team* D. Fox C. Gilbert Sister M. Hurst
1972–3	Feasibility trials were held in Staffordshire in six schools and a college of further education Twelve teachers and sixty students tried four Units Teachers recommended that the production of a wide choice of Units was needed before trials could begin	
1973–4	Writing teams were set up in Gloucestershire, Hertfordshire, Leicestershire, Manchester, and Staffordshire Writers included teachers who knew the needs of the students from firsthand experience The intention was to produce twenty Units for trial	*Organiser* Hilda Misselbrook *Team* C. P. Elliot D. Fox N. D. Stears J. C. Taylor D. Tomley K. Wild
1974–5	The Evaluator joined the team First year of the full trials began in over forty schools and colleges Fifteen Units were tried during the year Additional writing groups were set up in Leeds, Calderdale, Cheshire, Lancashire, Thames Valley, and Hampshire It was hoped that a total of forty Units could be produced	*Organiser* K. Wild *Evaluator* J. K. Gilbert *Team* C. P. Elliot Hilda Misselbrook N. D. Stears J. C. Taylor D. Tomley
1975–6	Second year of full trials was held in over seventy schools and colleges Additional Units were tried, bringing the total to thirty-eight full Units and several Mini-Units Revision of the first batch of Units began	
1976–7	Full trials had been completed; limited trials continued, of Units where there was not enough feedback Some new schools and colleges tried out materials Revision continued Publication of Units planned in three batches, in spring 1977, summer 1977, and winter 1978	

The full list of titles, below, gives some idea of the breadth of opportunities for working in a framework of science and reflects the richness which arises from stimulating teacher groups to devise teaching material for a wider audience than their own teaching groups. The Units have been produced essentially as a result of the initiatives of the teachers and with the assistance rather than the direction of the central team.

Air Pollution	*Food*	*Psychology*
Beyond Our Ken	*Football*	*Questioning Prejudice and*
Birds	*Gardening*	*Superstition*
Brewing	*Glass*	*Recycling*
Cosmetics	*Hair*	*Science Fiction*
Crime Detection	*Keeping the Heat*	*Slimming*
Efficiency	*In*	*Sport*
Electronics	*Mining and Min-*	*Survival*
Energy 2000	*erals*	*Study of a Local Industry*
Enterprise	*The Motor Car*	*Town and Country Trails*
Farming	*Noise*	*Understanding Old Age*
Feet and Footwear	*People and Roads*	*Water Pollution*
Fibres and Fabrics	*Photography*	*Water Shortage: 2000*
Fire	*Pottery*	*Weather*

The teachers also devised three booklets of Mini-Units, each intended to take two weeks to complete rather than the six to eight weeks required for a full Unit.

Mini-Units I	*Mini-Units II*	*Mini-Units III*
Boomerangs	Packaging	Parachutes
Dowsing	Paper Aeroplanes	Space Communications
Optical Illusions	Questionnaires	Stage Make-up
Recognising Pollution	Recycling Glass	The Strength of Concrete

Teachers' notes for each Unit and two teachers' guides were also written. The teachers in the schools not only determined the style of each Unit but also the style of response open to students. This may range from filmed reports, tape-slide sets, and exhibition displays to radio or newspaper reports as well as a file describing and recording the work done.

Perhaps the most interesting feature is that the project approach has spread far beyond the initial planning of the central team and a number of schools in England and Wales, without any direct link with the project and without any central funding, are busily producing their own curricula through parallel processes of in-school discussion to those adopted by the project. Thus Queen Mary College, Basingstoke, has produced a wholly school-developed curriculum unit on *Weather*. Thames Valley College, Richmond upon Thames, produced a unit on *Cosmetics* and a group of schools working together in Hebden Bridge, Yorkshire, produced an extensive curriculum package on the *Study of a Local Industry*.

The writing teams varied in size from one or two people to twenty or thirty. Most contained teachers in day-to-day contact with the students for whom the Unit is written and at least one who had expert knowledge of the topic. It is very helpful, sometimes essential, to have an 'outside' expert in the team. Failing this, it is vital to ensure that drafts of material will be seen by someone with up-to-date and detailed knowledge. All the writers remained in full-time posts and were often able to try out their ideas with appropriate students as writing progressed.

The writers met in teachers' centres, in one another's schools, in university or college Departments of Education, in pubs, in each other's homes, and at writing conferences. The three writing conferences were essential to hammer out a writing policy and to agree on a framework within which the units were written. Such decisions as listing the objectives in the students' guides, confining a section to not more than four sides of A4 paper, aiming at about two-thirds text and one-third visual material in a students' guide, and (with certain exceptions) restricting the teachers' notes for a Unit to four sides of A4 paper, were arrived at during work and discussion at the writing conferences. These decisions were later supported by the feedback from trials.

The Units were typed, illustrations were drawn and pasted in, and the required number of copies were run off, generally with simple reprographic machinery. Back-up materials such as slides, filmstrips, and tape recordings were produced and copied. After trials, the Units were revised in the light of feedback. They were then prepared for publication by a sub-editor, assisted by members of the original writing team.

Suggestions for titles of Units were received from teachers and students — a few hundred students responded to questionnaires on two occasions. Writers added their own ideas and the team kept an eye on the overall balance of subject and style in the growing list of titles. Some topics which were considered for inclusion during the trials but were not written are listed below. Several were suggested by students who were encouraged to put their ideas forward. Others were proposed by teachers and others interested in the project.

Adhesives	Disability	Printing
Advertising	First Aid	Pumps
Angling	Housing	Railways
Astronomy	Learning to Read	Safety
Brickmaking	Paint	Sailing
Building	Pets	Science for the Future
Communications	Politics	Timber

The project had completed its first task of producing a bank of Units by the summer of 1978 and it is intended to revise and up-date each Unit at the time it comes up for reprinting. There is no reason, however, why Units should not be added to the list from time to time. Figure 2.2 gives a scheme of how this could be done.

The Staffordshire Education Authority and the Education Department of the University of Keele have responded to the challenge in two ways. In the summer of 1977, some forty teachers produced Mini-Units on the following subjects during a four-day course at the University.

Canned Power	Into Focus	Protection from Radioactivity
Chicken or Egg	Kites	Solar Central Heating
Flight	Packaging an Egg	Stage Lighting
Human Behaviour	Paint	Wood Composites
	Projectiles	Work Study

More recently plans have been proposed to develop a Resources Centre and Curriculum Development Unit under the aegis of the Keele Science and Technology Centre. It may well be that further developments along the lines of Working with Science and Children Investigating will be one of the results of that initiative.

Assessment and evaluation

The Working with Science Project team tackled the problem of how to assess students' progress in a variety of ways and placed the emphasis on self-assessment. Each Unit contains clearly stated objectives of what the student could achieve and poses questions in the text to focus the mind of the student on these objectives. Further, each Unit contains an assessment instrument designed to help the student to ascertain how far the objectives listed in the Unit had, or had not, been realised. The project also emphasised assessment by the people interested in the work done: it is suggested that a panel of local people could give their approval to work submitted to them. This, in turn, could lead to local certificates being produced. In some schools and colleges the clamour of students for paper qualifications led their teachers to become involved with the pilot studies of the Certificate of Extended Education and many interesting and novel assessment schemes were devised during and after the field trials of the project materials.

Teacher evaluation of the project was encouraged and it was suggested that teachers complete the questionnaire below to guide and inform their own judgment.

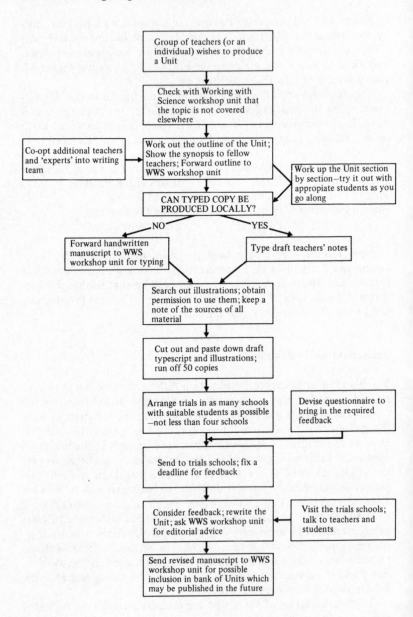

Figure 2.2 *Scheme for production of additional units*

PART A
Before deciding to use the materials

	Yes	No
The school or college has students:		
taking O-levels	☐	☐
retaking O-levels	☐	☐
with a light timetable	☐	☐
doing general studies	☐	☐
These students:		
would benefit from non-specialist science	☐	☐
ought to develop more outside interests	☐	☐
need ideas on future jobs	☐	☐
are capable, if given help, of making choices	☐	☐
The school or college has:		
most of the facilities for sciences at A-level	☐	☐
enough money to buy the Project materials	☐	☐
The science department is happy to see science as:		
a series of processes that students can apply	☐	☐
facts and ideas in which these students are interested	☐	☐
something that these students can be helped to learn	☐	☐
a subject for study by these students, working at their own pace	☐	☐
The science department has a clear policy on:		
methods of internal assessment of students' work	☐	☐
the usefulness of external examinations for these students	☐	☐

If the majority of answers are in the 'Yes' column, then the Working with Science materials can be used forthwith. But the implications of the 'No' answers must be considered.

PART B
Before using the materials with a class

	Yes	No
Is it possible to arrange:		
extended periods of time for the classes	☐	☐
for suitable staff to be available	☐	☐
for other staff to act as consultants	☐	☐
for the students to be available	☐	☐
for the use of a laboratory	☐	☐
access to other facilities, such as the gym	☐	☐
for the required books and equipment to be ready	☐	☐
for out-of-school/college visits	☐	☐

The Units to be made available to students:

make demands within the scope of the personal knowledge
of the staff □ □
are likely to appeal to this range of students □ □
are capable of being successfully done by the students □ □
require equipment that is available □ □

Examination of each of these Units has shown:

the aims and objectives to be met □ □
the content that is to be covered □ □
the activities involved □ □
what abilities and experience students will need □ □

Decisions have been taken on:

the strategy of introducing students to the Units □ □
the pattern of use of the Units □ □
how long to spend on each Unit □ □
the kinds of report required from students □ □

Guided student choice of Units will be based on:

a balance of subject types □ □
whether the student has the knowledge and ability to make
good use of the Unit □ □
the style of the material □ □
the view that the student has of science □ □
the previous experience of the student □ □

In this section, a majority of answers in the 'Yes' column indicates that a teacher is organized and ready to use the materials with a class. 'No' replies indicate, on the basis of experience in the trials, that difficulties will arise unless appropriate action is taken.

PART C
During the use of the materials

Yes No

In single periods students are:

organizing visits □ □
arranging to interview people □ □
writing up practical work □ □
ordering equipment for practicals □ □

In multiple-period lessons, students are:

away on visits □ □
doing practical work about the school or college □ □
doing practical work in the laboratory □ □

At home, students are:

writing reports on sections	□	□
doing out-of-school/college practical work	□	□
reading around and ahead of the topic	□	□

In classes, students spend an appropriate proportion of time:

working independently	□	□
working in groups	□	□
listening to a formal lesson	□	□

During classes, the teacher is:

organizing equipment	□	□
tutoring students on the material	□	□
demonstrating skills	□	□
helping students to select a Unit	□	□
keeping a record of students' progress	□	□
promoting independence in the students	□	□
balancing breadth and depth in students' work	□	□
giving students criteria for success in their work	□	□
supervising students' notes	□	□

It is well known that independent learning is most demanding of staff time, skills, insight, and organizing ability. A majority of answers 'Yes' indicates that things are probably going extremely well. But 'Nos' indicate a need for some change in emphasis.

PART D
After the materials have been used

	Yes	No
Students have become more:		
numerate	□	□
literate	□	□
knowledgeable about the physical environment	□	□
knowledgeable about the social environment	□	□
willing to assume moral responsiblity	□	□
ready to respond aesthetically	□	□
willing to use the methods of science	□	□
practised in the skills of science	□	□
capable of self-organization	□	□
capable of independent learning	□	□

The evaluation of the project during final trials was undertaken by an evaluator with the active help of the organiser and the area co-ordinators. Careful attention was paid to the professional judgment of the teachers and to the opinions of the students. Questionnaires, visits and free response correspondence were used in the evaluation. A group of teachers at a writing conference was asked for views on what could reasonably and realistically be asked of teachers and students. This led to a battery of five one-page inquiries; a background questionnaire seeking basic facts about the school or college; a teacher and a student questionnaire to collect feedback on each Unit; a student general questionnaire to provide information on the achievements, aspirations and current course of each student; and a teacher general questionnaire to inquire about the place of materials in the school curriculum, students' performance in the method skills and attitudes of science, and the strategies associated with the use of the project materials. The evaluation report on each Unit contained an analysis of questionnaire data, a digest of all written comment arranged in categories, and a commentary on how each Unit was received. These reports were sent to the editors responsible for rewriting the Units. They were discussed with the original writing teams and taken into account in rewriting the Unit. The reports on visits and on the general questionnaires were used to inform the writing of the teachers' guides.

Chapter 3

Continuing curriculum change at Codsall School

Paul Abbs

Codsall High School is a mixed 13–18 comprehensive with 959 students on roll, of which 149 are in the Sixth Form, and with the equivalent of 61.5 teaching staff in the September of 1978. It serves the residential villages of Codsall and Bilbrook and surrounding rural areas and lies some six miles north-west of Wolverhampton. Although the catchment area has close links with Wolverhampton and the West Midlands conurbation for employment, shopping, entertainment and other services it lies within the south-west corner of the county of Staffordshire. It is somewhat isolated from other Staffordshire secondary schools and the nearest Local Authority Teachers' Centres are at Lichfield and Stone, both some twenty miles distant. The original school, a mixed secondary modern, was opened in 1940. When the school became an 11–18 comprehensive in September 1969 a new clasp block was added and three years later a further wing was built. The campus also accumulated its fair share of 'huts' and mobile classrooms. The governing body has given the school good support, but in terms of the curriculum has for the most part placed particular emphasis on good examination results, traditional subject teaching and streaming. Many of the more articulate parents have put considerable pressure on the school to enter their children for O-level rather than CSE and to increase the amount of homework.

The Local Authority advisers and officers serve the school well and are readily available for advice when requested but, with the exception of science, there has been no sustained curriculum development in collaboration with other Authority secondary schools. The school has good relationships with and regularly takes students for teaching practice from the Education Departments of the Universities of Birmingham and Keele, the Wolverhampton Polytechnic, West Midlands College of Education and, formerly, also from Madeley and Dudley Colleges of Education. These institutions, except for Wolverhampton Polytechnic, which has only recently expanded its Education Faculty, are fairly distant for easy contact and no continuous dialogue over curricular questions has occurred. The curriculum innovations and developments which have taken place in the school have been almost entirely dependent on the knowledge and expertise of the teaching staff. I have very briefly placed the school in its ecological setting, and before giving some details of recent curricular changes I will outline the historical background of the last decade, a decade of considerable change.

In September 1969 the school received its first comprehensive intake under a new Head, Mr R. Mitson. He and Mr M. Holder, who was appointed as Head of Upper School and Resources Adviser, were prime movers in building up a Resource Centre and advocating school-based resource development. Detailed accounts of the workings of the Centre appear in Schools Council Working Paper 43, *School Resource Centres*,[1] and in Norman Beswick's book *Organizing Resources.*[2] In January 1973 Mr Mitson left for his new post as Principal of Abraham Moss Centre, Manchester, to be followed later in the year by Mr Holder and also the Assistant Head of Resources, Mr Hill. Mrs White, the teacher-librarian, moved to Cheshire where her husband had gained promotion. Thus in just over six months all the key personnel in the development of the Resource Centre had left. Mr G. Bate, the former Deputy, obtained the Headship. The school was at a critical stage. The first uncreamed comprehensive intake was about to reach the Fifth Year and all the detailed planning for the expansion of the Sixth Form had still to be carried out. The natural growth of the school and changes in Burnham created two new posts at Deputy Head level. Mr Bate designed two complementary job specifications, one for a Director of Administration and one for a Director of Studies. In the brief of the latter was included:

(i) the stimulation of curriculum awareness and innovation amongst teaching staff
(ii) the direction and co-ordination of all team and integrated studies
(iii) the direction and co-ordination of the resources centre, the multi-media library and teacher support services
(iv) the organisation of in-service training and associated activities for the staff of the school
(v) the co-ordination of teaching practice arrangements and liaison with local colleges of education and university departments

These were some of the tasks that I had to face in the September of 1973 and it is mainly on my role that I shall concentrate my remarks. The third person of Deputy status was the longest serving member of the staff, Miss Orton, who was Senior Mistress and who had responsibilities for time-tabling, for all administration concerned with internal and external examinations, for day-to-day communications and staff cover. All three posts were of equal status and involved responsibilities for development and planning of the school.

During the three years from September 1973 the school continued to grow in size. Growth brings many advantages. It should stimulate staff to think through and plan their courses from first principles and it brings new allowances and posts thereby enabling the school to appoint new staff and create new roles. It should necessitate a reappraisal of the procedures for decision-making and communication, as well as routine administration. On the other hand it also brought about an acute accommodation crisis. The school had settled down for only one year as an all-through 11–18 comprehensive when it had to meet the challenge of further reorganisation, this time three tier. During the two years following September 1975, which was the last year for an intake at 11, the school contracted by over 500 pupils. Some staff who left could not be replaced and many departments were anxious about overstaffing. Whereas expansion brings opportunities, contraction is rather a painful process. The more talented and ambitious teachers tend to leave and at the level of middle management often cannot be replaced. The first new intake from two new 9–13 middle schools joined the high school in September 1978.

During my five years at the school the main staff preoccupations and energies have been focused on the comprehensive intake entering the Fifth Year and taking public examinations, and the subsequent expansion and development of a comprehensive Sixth Form. For the last two years the preparations for and implications of three-tier reorganisation have been uppermost in teachers' minds. In addition, throughout the period Mr Bate has made every endeavour to develop and promote the community dimension of the school. Three years ago a magnificent new sports complex, shared with the community, was added to the existing youth centre and evening institute.

The events which I have briefly sketched are the backdrop to the curricular changes which I will now analyse in more detail. I wish to make it clear that the perspective I adopt is that of a Deputy with curricular responsibilities and any critical comments I express are my own personal interpretations and views. At the centre of curricular development is what happens in classrooms and in other learning situations but I will in this short account be largely restricting myself to observations on curricular structures, organisation and support systems. Of course, the wider aspects of school life are of no less importance, particularly the school's philosophy towards the personal well-being of the student. Dr T. Brown, the Director of Administration, has done much to encourage enlightened policies. For instance, a pastoral structure has been developed that in essence is concerned with the nature of the relationships that exist between all parties in school. This has included staff participation in establishing a clear policy towards rewards and sanctions, developing ways of dealing with difficult and disruptive pupils and a steadily expanding policy of parental contact through home visiting. A well-co-ordinated careers programme exists and a health education course is, at present, under review. Attempts have been made to establish a School Council through which pupils can participate in the running of the school. So far the measure has not attracted the 60 per cent staff majority felt to be necessary for successful implementation. On any controversial issue, a staff majority is not only desirable for staff cohesion but necessary if goodwill is to be obtained during the implementation of an innovation or new practice.

For school-based curriculum development to be successful I believe that the perspectives of the curriculum theorists and specialists have to be brought into meaningful dialogue with the day-to-day practice of teachers. At present, unfortunately, there too often exists a credibility gap between the world of the teacher with its immediate pressures, and that of the academic, researcher, adviser and curriculum developer. Reference to epistemology, sociology of knowledge, illuminative evaluation and phenomenology, to mention only a few important perspectives, embarrasses most teachers. Yet grasp of theory is essential. The teacher who most claims to eschew theory and to be commonsensical and pragmatic in his approach is in most need of critical insight into his basic assumptions. An organised programme of systematic evaluation and development is required in each school and if this is to be rigorous and constructive sufficient time must be provided. I return to this critical point at the end of this essay. I draw heavily in the remaining overview on extracts that have been produced in this school. I have tried to keep these as simple as possible and have made little or no reference to specific educational research, reports and writings, though my debt to these is enormous.

When I joined the school in September 1973 the school was grouped into Upper, Middle and Lower bands with three parallel classes in each band, but for certain subjects — Art, Technical, Home Economics, Physical Education and programmes of team teaching in the Humanities — groups were mixed-ability. The team teaching involved Inter-Disciplinary Enquiry (IDE) in the first two years, where Bruner's *Man: a Course of Study* (MACOS) formed a sizeable proportion of the course, Community Studies in the Third Year and English, General and Social Studies in the Fourth and Fifth Years. In the first two years History and Religious Education did not appear on the time-table as separate categories, in the Third Year Community Studies was an extra course, taken by all except for a small minority who were taking a third Foreign Language, Russian or Latin; while in the Fourth and Fifth Year all students took English, General and Social Studies, which involved one-fifth of the available time in a six-day time-table. Usually a whole year group of over 200 students or half a year group were block time-tabled and an open plan area adjacent to the multi-media library was used as the main teaching base. The teachers involved were time-tabled for a planning period in school time and most teams had an extra member of staff, the 'floater', who could be deployed in a variety of ways. These courses in the Humanities were integrated, mixed-ability, team taught and resource based, characteristics which have a certain logical inter-relationship and which, in principle, I fully favour. However, in the autumn of 1973 there were tremendous difficulties. Most of the key personnel who had set up the courses had left, most of the teachers allocated to the teams were new to the school and to the practice of team teaching, no existing staff had specific responsibilities for co-ordination and no Heads of Department had control of content. There was neither vertical integration between IDE, Community Studies and English, General and Social Studies nor co-ordination between the disciplines of History, Geography, Religious Education and English, where these appeared on the time-table as separate subjects, and the integrated courses. To some extent I gained the impression that the courses had been devised to serve the development of the Resource Centre.

Teams were under great pressure to produce teaching materials and to structure learning situations in time for the week's lessons. In the Fifth Year all the materials had still to be produced and in other years previous topics, themes and teaching materials were often not thought to be suitable. The teams were existing from hand to mouth. What was to be taught next week, how and with what materials were pressing questions. The teachers involved were in the front line and there was not sufficient time for long-term planning, strategy and evaluation. It usually fell to one or two committed staff to write the teaching material, including guides for teachers, student material and work tasks and to collate resources. Once drafted, any print material was soon processed and duplicated by the Resource Centre into attractive booklets and sheets, the staple diet of the courses. There was little time for team discussion of the materials. It is a thoroughly worthwhile exercise for a teacher to write his own material, to arrange content, to lay bare its conceptual contours and to set his own questions and tasks for students. The materials can be reconstructed to meet the teacher's requirements for his students in their particular situation. Such an approach is extremely flexible and given the back-up of a sophisticated resource centre the teaching materials can be as attractively packaged as most commercial items. Nor need material be restricted to the print format. But there are drawbacks. It is very time consuming and one doubts whether under existing teaching loads teachers can spend so many hours burning the midnight oil in preparing materials and at the same time carry out their other teaching functions as effectively as they might. In a team-teaching situation without sufficient time for critical scrutiny, discussion and ideally for trial testing and, where necessary, rewriting, a teacher's home-produced materials can be just as alien and uninviting as many textbooks and commercial packs for the other teachers in the team. Consequently there is the danger that the materials will be used unintelligently and ineffectively by team members in the classroom. There are no teacher-proof learning resources, at least in schools where attendance is compulsory.

One aspect of resource-based learning is to provide individualised learning programmes and to give students access to learning materials in all kinds of formats and media. But an inherent contradiction of team teaching is that block time-tabling with large numbers is desirable for lead lessons, for films and other visual presentations, for visiting speakers, for visits and fieldwork, and for the opportunity to rotate groups among specialist staff, but for the greater part of the time, when students are engaged in discussion, written work and inquiry, easy access to the whole range of resources is required, and unfortunately large numbers can result in bottlenecks in the supply of resources, both of hardware and software, and hence frustrate attempts to promote independent learning. In the team teaching lessons students were in such large numbers that though the multi-media library made every facility available to them, their legitimate requests for audio-tapes, slides, books, working collections, extracts and other resources could not satisfactorily be met and overcrowding became a problem in the library. Thus most students for most of the time worked their way through teacher-produced workbooks. This critique is not intended to undermine such approaches to teaching and learning but to point out that if such schemes are to be successful more time, more resources and more space are necessary and teachers must be clear in their minds about aims, pupil assessment and evaluation procedures. Some outside comment was made at the time as to whether Codsall Resource Centre could survive such a massive turnover of staff. Events have shown that the Centre developed and expanded. It was the curriculum which was to undergo considerable reconstruction.

As I have indicated, each of the various teams led virtually an independent existence and except for my brief there was no overall framework for co-ordination and planning. Apart from the teams and the Resource Centre Committee, which had only come to meet on a regular basis at Mr Bate's instigation, the sole organised meeting at the time for discussing curricular matters in detail was a large and loose federation of departments. There had been previously in Mr Mitson's time a Curriculum Group Meeting which had discussed specific curricular issues. My intentions early in the autumn term of 1973 were to rationalise the curriculum, to create a common core of studies throughout the compulsory years of schooling, to group 'the federation of departments' into a faculty system and establish an Academic Board. The philosophical underpinnings for such changes rested on the work of the London philosophers of education, Peters, Hirst and — most influential at the time in shaping my thinking — White, and the arguments he develops in his book *Towards a Compulsory Curriculum.*[3] The Head and other Deputies were sympathetic to these broad aims. Indeed, Dr Brown was in the process of rationalising the pastoral structure and defining roles more clearly.

At the first meeting of the 'federation of departments' there were some thirty-odd teachers, every teacher in the school with one or more scale points with responsibilities for some area of the curriculum. I was of the opinion that there had to be structural changes because a group of this size was too large for detailed discussion and planning and because so many teachers representing some thirty different subject areas and competing against each other for a place on the time-table would not facilitate any moves towards a 'common core'. Any restructuring of the curriculum in an existing institution causes uncertainty and anxiety, for a teacher's subject status and even livelihood are threatened. At the meeting I outlined my arguments for a faculty structure. The major arguments were that definite and distinct areas of knowledge could be distinguished, that a faculty structure should reflect these and that a small group, made up of members each with a major responsibility for a main sector of the curriculum, should form an academic board. Minor arguments were that in a large institution it was administratively tidier and more convenient for such routine matters as time-tabling, capitation, examination entries and induction of new staff to have a simplified structure and that recent Burnham awards meant major faculty posts could be matched with appropriate remuneration on scale IV. There was general agreement as to the validity of these arguments but hardly enthusiasm, for many at the meeting who wanted to be involved would clearly not have a place on the Academic Board.

In addition to the Heads of Mathematics and English there was already a Head of Science, Foreign Languages and Physical Education. On the existing staff there were Heads of Art, Home Economics and Technical of comparable status and all three obtained a place on the new Heads of Faculty. An appointment was sought from outside to co-ordinate the existing work of the Departments of History, Geography, Social Studies and Sociology, to promote Economics and to develop IDE. Business Studies, not a distinct realm of knowledge but a very successful and popular department in the upper part of the school, and Religious Education and Music, both small but distinctive departments, were also to be represented on the new committee. These decisions were taken by the executive or senior management team, comprising Head, Deputies and Senior Teachers. The faculty structure that finally emerged is outlined in Table 3.1.

TABLE 3.1 *Faculty structure*

Mathematics	Computing Studies
English	Language, Literature
Foreign Languages	French, German, Russian, Latin, European Studies
Social Sciences	History, Geography, Economics, Sociology, Environmental Studies, Social Studies, IDE and Bruner
Science	Physics, Chemistry, Biology, Rural Science, Nuffield Science, Integrated Science, Combined Science, Environmental Science
Design and Creative Technology	(i) Art, Pottery, Photography (ii) Metalwork, Woodwork, Engineering Drawing/Technical Drawing exploration materials (iii) Home Economics, Needlework, Crafts
Music	Music, choir, orchestra
Moral and Religious Education	Religious Studies
Business Studies	Typing, Pitmanscript, Commerce, Office Practice, Shorthand
Recreational activities	PE, sport, games, dance, outside activities, etc.

At the same period a framework for handling the decision-making process throughout the school was established. Details of the arrangements are given in Figure 3.1, which is taken from the staff handbook, compiled by Dr Brown. Regular faculty/departmental meetings and Heads of Faculty meetings thus interlinked gave regular opportunities for raising issues, discussion and powers of decision-making, subject only to the approval of the Head and the senior management group. Each faculty was given autonomy to the extent that its policies and practices did not impinge on the work of other faculties and the general running of the school.

The first task of the newly formed Heads of Faculty board was to review the existing curricular structure and to examine the feasibility of extending a common core of studies in the Fourth and Fifth years to replace some of the existing option pools. A document was produced entitled 'Fourth and Fifth Year curriculum: some proposals for your consideration', which was intended to initiate discussion and stimulate thinking at the Heads of Faculty meetings. (And see Figure 3.2.)

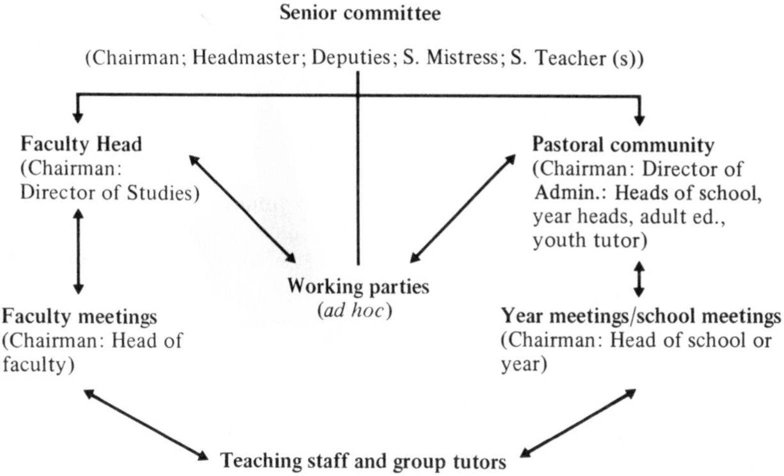

Senior committee

(Chairman; Headmaster; Deputies; S. Mistress; S. Teacher (s))

Faculty Head
(Chairman:
Director of Studies)

Pastoral community
(Chairman: Director of
Admin.: Heads of school,
year heads, adult ed.,
youth tutor)

Working parties
(*ad hoc*)

Faculty meetings
(Chairman: Head of
faculty)

Year meetings/school meetings
(Chairman: Head of school or
year)

Teaching staff and group tutors

Figure 3.1 *Decision-making processes*

1 Regular minuted meetings of Year Groups and Faculties (or depart-ments) are held.
2 The Faculty Heads meet on the third Thursday of each month and the Pastoral Heads on the fourth Thursday.
3 Departmental meetings are generally held on the first Thursday, and Year Group meetings on the second Thursday of each month.
4 The Headmaster, Deputies and Senior Mistress meet each week.
5 The senior management group above and the Head of School meet as necessary.
6 Staff meetings are held mainly for information and to 'air' views on particular issues. Sometimes staff are 'expected' to attend, other meetings are 'open', with attendance voluntary.

It is intended that all staff are involved in arriving at decisions. Any particular item should be discussed at year group/department level, and views represented at the Pastoral/Faculty Heads meeting. The Senior Staff will generally ratify and implement decisions taken by the pastoral/faculty committees. It depends on the issue, but it may be necessary to set up working parties or hold a staff meeting, for example, prior to the final decision.

As there is a large staff, it is possible that the intention of staff parti-cipation and involvement falls short of the ideal. If this does happen, would staff please approach one of the senior staff as quickly as possible.

Fourth and Fifth Year curriculum:
some proposals for your consideration

Some objectives:
  (i) to provide a balanced education for all students, preventing premature specialisation and hence allowing options to be left open for the Sixth Form and Higher and Further Education
 (ii) to offer all students the central modes of thinking and feeling (domains or realms of knowledge) in a common core
(iii) to offer an intellectually stimulating and demanding curriculum for all students and to develop the diverse talents and aspirations of everyone
 (iv) to provide where possible block time-tabling to allow team-teaching and flexibility, e.g. to permit mixed ability grouping, to postpone the time for the final selection for 'O' level, to permit transfer between C.S.E. and 'O' level groups, etc.
  (v) to encourage the construction of common objectives, content and methods of assessment for 'O' level and C.S.E. in each subject area in preparation for a common exam at 16+.

I was uncertain as to whether Foreign Languages should be in the core and had ambivalent attitudes towards the importance and even existence of vocational courses, usually geared to the less able, at this stage of education. The Head of Foreign Languages put forward such a strong case for her faculty and was prepared to take all students by providing a whole range of courses, including two Mode 3 European Studies courses, that her request was essentially met. On purely intellectual grounds my reservations remain because Foreign Languages are not a 'form or realm' of knowledge and many of the concepts, skills and much of the body of knowledge incorporated in European Studies courses can in many cases be handled more competently by Social Science teachers. However, in the particular context of a school, such philosophical considerations have to be modified by the democratic process, pragmatism and realism. In a similar vein, my personal belief is that comprehensive schools should provide a genuine secondary education for all students. Hence to offer practical and vocational courses, which in practice are taken by those students who are considered to be non-academic, is divisive, undermining the intrinsic value of education and prematurely channels such students into certain sectors of the labour market. Due to environmental and parental influences and the legacy of selective schooling such courses are popular with many working-class students. On such courses they can readily see the relevance of what they are doing and they are engaging in 'real' work. As with Foreign Languages a compromise solution was reached. The principle of a core not only for English, Mathematics and Physical Education, common to most schools, but also for at least one creative or design subject, one social science and for about 70 per cent of the intake some work in a foreign language was clearly established, as the outcome of prolonged discussions. Science emerged with two 'cores' and in addition there were two option pools enabling students to develop particular talents or interests and to specialise. The integrated scheme for English, General and Social Studies was greatly altered. English became a core taught by specialists. Sociology and Social Studies lost its monopoly position and had to compete with Economics, History and Religious Studies, and specific time for General Studies was squeezed out.

Democratic discussion, but with real influence vested in the Heads of Faculty meeting, resulted in a more specialist curriculum in the Humanities. There was also considerable animosity expressed at the time both towards planning time for the teams being on the time-table and towards the open-plan teaching area. Both in the following year were to disappear. As with many other groups in modern society, teachers are very concerned about differential working conditions and status. A second and more convincing argument was that planning time in school hours resulted in larger teaching groups across the curriculum. The open-plan area was disliked by many staff because insufficient teacher control could be exercised when large groups (often over 100 students) were working in the area. By the beginning of the following academic year the area had been converted into four conventional classrooms and the extension to the library became a Sixth Form private study area. Mixed-ability teaching groups were introduced into the First Year and an extra First Year class was created to bring down group sizes. The first comprehensive intake into the Sixth Form resulted in the proliferation of smaller teaching groups at the top end of the school and the teams, as formerly constituted for English, General and Social Studies, because of changes in the curriculum, were phased out. These changes meant that team planning did not appear on the time-table.

The details of the whole curriculum for 1975 are given in the diagrams. These are almost identical to the pattern for 1974. The 1975 structure is outlined because that is the first year when all year groups were based on a comprehensive intake. The common core in the Fourth and Fifth Years is outlined in Figure 3.3 and the two option blocks in Figure 3.4. To complete the picture, years one to three are shown in Table 3.2, the Sixth-Form examination courses are summarised in Table 3.3 and the programme of General Education in Table 3.4.

The new faculty structure and decision-making procedures throughout the school were soon institutionalised. The structure of the whole curriculum had been overhauled and a common core in the Fourth and Fifth Years had been implemented, anticipating by four years several recommendations in the Green Paper *Education in Schools: A Consultative*

10 periods
Humanities

English Language
English Literature
Moral and Religious Education
Social Studies/Sociology
includes Careers, Sex Education
Health Education, etc.

10 periods
Mathematics/Science

(4–6 or 5–5 breakdown?)
Physics
Chemistry
Biology
Integrated Courses

———— Project Technology? ————

4 periods
Creative Technology

Art, Metalwork
Woodwork, Home
Economics, Needlework,
Music, etc.

2 periods
Physical Education

+ 2 periods choice
(i) Physical Education or
dance, or (ii) options from
creative technology and
drama, or (iii) minority
subjects, e.g. Russian*

Options: three blocks each with 4 periods. Students select one from each

I	II	III
French	History	French
German	Geography	German
Latin	Business Studies	Environmental Science
European Studies	Art	Biology
Technical Drawing	Home Economics	Geography
Living Today	Metalwork	Business Studies

(other subjects could be added to these options)

This scheme permits 8 subjects for all, 9 with English
Literature, 10 in special circumstances with a minority subject

N.B. 1 No group in common core and options ought to have less
than 16 students, around the 24 mark desirable
2 Minority subjects attracting few candidates to be resource-
based individual learning (Open University style) with tutorial
help perhaps in one of the tutor group periods or as above*

Figure 3.2 *Common core based on a five-day week with forty periods for Fourth and Fifth years: an outline model
and some proposals for your consideration*

All students take: English
Mathematics
Physical Education

Humanities

English	*Social Science*	*Creative Technology*	*Science*		*European Studies*

You all You select one subject from: | You select one subject from: | You select two subjects one from each column: | | You select one subject from:
take

English	*Social Science*	*Creative Technology*	*Science*		*European Studies*
English	1 History (Economic & Social)	1 Art			
	2 Religious Studies	2 Eng. Drawing	1	2	1 French
	3 Sociology and Social Studies	3 Home Economics			2 German
	4 Social Economics	4 Needlework (dress)	Integrated Science	(double O-level) 1 group	3 European Studies (Mode 3 CSE)
		5 Metalwork	Combined Science	(double CSE) 2 groups	4 European Studies (non-linguistic Mode 3 CSE)
		6 Woodwork	Biology	Biology	
			Chemistry (CSE)	Chemistry	
			Home Economics	Geography	
			Link Course		
			Physics (O-level)	Physics (CSE)	
			Rural Science (CSE)	Rural Science	
			Living with Science (CSE)		

Link Course Engineering Technology

Those taking Building or Home Management Course ⟶

∨ ∨

Instead of one Science and Creative Technology

Do not take a Science from Column 2 or European Studies

Courses
Building Course, Automobile and Electrical Engineering and Technical Studies Course — 16 periods a week.
Home Management, Crafts and Child Care Course — 16 periods a week.
Students opting for this do *not* take European Studies, a second science and subjects from the two option blocks.

Figure 3.3 *Fourth and Fifth Year curriculum: plan of the common core for September 1975*

Curriculum change at Codsall School

Option 1
One subject from:

1 Art
2 Biology (O-level only)
3 Commerce
4 Engineering Drawing (Link Course must opt for this)
5 English Literature (O-level only)
6 Geography
7 Latin
8 Music
9 Typing

Option 2
One Subject from:

1 French
2 Geography
3 German
4 History
5 Metalwork
6 Needlework
7 Office Practice
8 Typing

Courses

Building Course, Automobile and Electrical Engineering and Technical Studies Course – 16 periods a week.

Home Management, Crafts and Child Care Course – 16 periods a week.

Students opting for this do *not* take European Studies, a second science and subjects from the two option blocks.

Figure 3.4 *Fourth and Fifth Year curriculum: plan of two option blocks*

TABLE 3.2 *Curriculum in Years 1–3: Codsall Comprehensive, September 1975*

Subject		1st Year	2nd Year	3rd Year
Mathematics		5	5	5
French		5	5	5
Science		5	5	5
English		5	5	5
History	IDE to			2 (Hist.)
	include Bruner's	6	6	
Geography	MACOS course			2 (Geog.)
Religious Studies		2	2	1
Creative Technology		6	6	6
Music		2	2	1
PE		4	4	4
German or Latin		–	–	4 or
Environmental Studies/Typing or Technical Drawing and Computing Studies		–	–	4
Total		40 periods	40 periods	40 periods

TABLE 3.3 *Sixth-form curriculum main courses: Examination courses to GCE Advanced and Ordinary Levels*

Advanced Level

Option 1	Option 2	Option 3	Option 4
English	Biology	Art	English
French	Economics	Chemistry	Geography
	Engineering Drawing	History	Latin
		Home Economics	Music
Mathematics	Further Maths		Physics
	German		
	Needlework		
	Religious Studies		
	Sociology		
8 periods	8 periods	8 periods	8 periods

Students select subjects from 3 option blocks (in some cases 2 or 1).
Students have private study when not taking a subject.
Where groups are very small a subject may have less than 8 periods a week.

One year O-level course

Mathematics	English Lit.	Human Biology	Social Economics	English Lang.
4 periods	4 periods	4 periods	4 periods	4 periods

These subjects can be taken at CSE.
Other O-levels that are required will be taken with Fifth Year O-level groups or in general options.

Business Studies Course

Commerce, Typing, Office Practice, Accounts, Shorthand to various levels can be taken as a complete course or, in part, in conjunction with A-level and O-level courses.

71

TABLE 3.4 'Sixth-form curriculum: General Studies

Common core General Studies	Physical Education	General Options*
2 periods	2 periods	
A study of general themes using inter-disciplinary approaches. Visits Speakers Debates Films etc.	Double period of Minor Games or Major Games	Art/Art Theory Computing and Electronics Comparative/Religion/ Philosophy Cooking/Homecrafts Drama/Play Reading English Literature French German Latin Mathematics/Statistics Photography Pitmanscript/Typing Music 16+ Science Sociology/World Affairs Workshop Technology

* There will be two option blocks, each with a double period. It is hoped to include the following subjects and activities in either one block or both. Students can alter their choices at the beginning of each term.

You will be able to take a further double period of games with the Second Year Sixth instead of one of these options, if you so wish.

Teaching staff will give you more detail of these subjects at the beginning of the Autumn Term.

There may be minor alterations to this pattern from term to term, depending on availability of teachers and on your option choices.

Document.[4] The 'teams' in the Humanities in the upper part of the school had undergone drastic changes, an unintended consequence from my point of view of the developments that had taken place. From one or two younger members of staff, committed to the 'teams', came remarks to the effect that enlightened despotism can provide more progressive policies than Heads of Faculty with vested interests to protect.

During subsequent years the curricular structures have been annually reviewed and slight modifications made. Alterations were made to the Third Year curriculum in readiness for the first intake from the two new middle schools in the September of 1978. The existing Third Year curriculum is shown in Figure 3.5. In the Fourth and Fifth Years, science

Subject	Periods per week
Mathematics	5
English	5
French	4
Science	6
Social Science Religious and Moral Education	6
Art	2
Music	2
Physical Education	4
Option	6
Total	40

Details of option

Choice of 1 or 2 or 3 of the following up to a total of 6 periods:

Home Economics:	Home Economics and Needlework	6
	Home Economics	2
	Needlework	2
Technical:	Engineering Drawing	2
	Metalwork	2
	Woodwork	2
	Technical Studies	2
Business Studies:	Typing	2
Second Foreign Language	German or Latin	4

Figure 3.5 *Curriculum: Codsall High School, foundation year 1978*

has been reduced from two 'cores' to one, but one of the option pools is now largely made up of science subjects and the aim is to achieve a situation where about 70 per cent of the year take up at least two science subjects. English and Mathematics now have increased time allocations (six periods) and English Literature is now an integral part of the English core and has disappeared as a separate option. To enable gifted scientists and linguists to take three sciences and two languages or the converse and to widen option choice generally an extended day class in a science or foreign language is offered each year. As a developing community school we would wish to extend this practice but at present any extra class outside normal school hours has to be time-tabled from our existing staff quota. Under these arrangements any expansion of this desirable practice would have deleterious effects on the size of groups during the normal school day. Details of the blocking arrangements, this time in the form of the sheet distributed to all students and their parents, are shown below.

Codsall High School   Summer 1978

Fourth and Fifth Year subject and course choices

Name (in full)   Tutor Group

Remember: (1) To discuss the possible choices with your parents, tutor, subject and career teachers.
　　　　　 (2) To study the handbook for details.
　　　　　 (3) Not to be influenced by what your friends do. It is your future that matters. What are the best choices for you?

Choose one subject or course from each section and state that choice in the place indicated. Please see handbook for details.

Common core
You all take English, Mathematics and Physical Education

1　Science core

　Biology   State choice here:
　Chemistry
　Combined Science (double CSE)
　Combined Science (single CSE)
　Physics
　Link (Car Maintenance)
　Link (Engineering Technology)
N.B. If you choose a Link course you must take a Science in Option block 1

2　Creative Technology core

　Art   State choice here:
　Engineering Drawing
　Home Economics
　Metalwork
　Music
　Needlework
　Woodwork
　Link (Car Maintenance)
　Link (Engineering Technology)

---

3 Social Science core

Geography   State choice here:
Social and Economic History (16+)
Social Economics
Social Studies/Sociology
Commerce

---

4 Foreign languages and European Studies core

French   State choice here:
German
European Studies (French) CSE
European Studies (German) CSE
*Building crafts
*Metalwork
*Typing
(N.B. * All do language courses where advised by Foreign
Languages Faculty)

---

5 Option block 1

Basic skills   State choice here:
Biology
Chemistry
Combined Science (double CSE)
Computer Studies CSE
Engineering Drawing
Geography (CSE)
Latin (for those beginning)
Metalwork
Office Practice
Physics
Rural Studies CSE
Typing

---

6 Option block 2

Art   State choice here:
Basic skills
Child care CSE
Engineering Drawing (Link must opt for this)
French
Geography
German
History 16+
Latin (for those already taking this subject)

Extended day

To enable students to extend their options a Physics O-level will be offered after school between 3.30 and 4.30 p.m. on two days a week You must be very committed to the subject and be able to cope with the extra work load. If you wish to take Physics, after school, state here:

Yes or No

Future job/career

If you have any ideas at this stage, please state.
Careers staff will be able to give you guidance.

Observations

If you wish to make any comments please make brief observations here:

All staff will be available for consultations on Parents' Evenings on 9th and 11th May.

Please fill in carefully and return BOTH forms to your group tutor by Monday 15th May.

Thank you
P. Abbs (Director of Studies)

Signed   Signed
(Student)   (Parent/Guardian)

This document is accompanied by a handbook giving details of subjects and courses. Pupils have the scheme explained to them as part of a careers programme and a meeting is held for parents where the rationale behind the scheme and the nature and the consequences of the choices to be made are discussed. A further parents' evening is then held where parents can discuss progress of individual students with teaching staff and general concerns with senior and careers staff.

Once the new curricular and management infrastructures had been established early in the academic year 1973-4, other issues could be reviewed and discussed and modifications to existing policies and practices carried out. Dr Brown and myself were both keen to see mixed-ability groupings introduced in the First Year into as many subject areas as were prepared to accept this development. As this was a controversial area, it was considered that the best way to introduce the proposal was at a special staff meeting. I prepared a short paper in summary form to initiate the discussion.

The case for mixed-ability grouping

Some arguments and points in favour of mixed-ability grouping:

1 The self-fulfilling prophecy. Pupils respond to some extent to the expectations of teachers and so when they are labelled A stream, C stream or E stream, or top band or bottom band, they will soon adapt themselves to the expected standard.
2 Pupils in low streams or bands feel a sense of failure, have a poor self-image and are not well motivated.
3 There is no fair criteria by which pupils can be allocated to streams. The 11+ and I.Q. tests are largely discredited if they are used for selection purposes.
4 As our pupils come from several different Primaries, which are largely unstreamed, there is a pragmatic argument against streaming in the first year.
5 There is little point changing from a Secondary Modern/ Grammar system to a Comprehensive system if the school is going to group pupils according to academic ability from the start.
6 Academic streaming is usually influenced not just by ability but also by behaviour, social class of pupils (large concentration of working-class pupils in lower streams), date of birth and other factors.
7 In streamed classes there are individual differences but these tend to get ignored in schools where streaming is practised.
8 With unstreaming there is less pre-judgement on pupils' ability and potential.
9 In unstreamed schools there is less anxiety among children. In particular, moving downstream is psychologically distressing.
10 No evidence that bright children are held back but some evidence that there is improvement in the academic performance of the average and less able pupils in unstreamed schools.
11 General agreement that there is better behaviour, more positive attitude to work and school and a more friendly atmosphere in unstreamed schools. 'Sink' classes with a concentration of all a year group's awkward, disturbed and less able pupils are done away with. There is also more likelihood of social mixing.
12 Evidence that more children stay on after the school leaving age and that examination results are better in unstreamed schools.

Preparing for the change

1 Important that the reasons for the change are clear and understood.
2 Teachers' attitudes, beliefs and commitment are vitally important.

3 Time and effort will need to be given to planning for the change.
4 Opportunity to think out afresh the objectives and content of your curriculum.
5 Teaching methods will need to be modified and changed if the move to mixed ability grouping is going to be successful.
6 We are fortunate in having the support services of a Resources Centre.

Some approaches for teaching mixed-ability classes

1 Where common material is taught it is desirable that this is structured:
   (a) simple beginning, with diagrams and illustrations where possible, for the average child;
   (b) a sophisticated tail and additional sheets and programmes of work for the more able.
2 Teachers set up learning situation — the desirability of more resource-based learning, discovery and individual enquiry.
3 Greater use of audio-visual equipment for class, group and individual work.
4 Teachers sharing ideas and materials and co-operating in various forms of team teaching.
5 Greater pupil involvement and say in what they do — where possible a choice of work.
6 Small group work and discussions — with the more able helping those with learning difficulties.
7 Different forms of assessment required. More detailed and sophisticated forms of continuous assessment, based on each child's ability and potential, are called for.
8 Withdrawal for remedial help where reading age below 9 in some academic subjects.

Faculties were given the opportunity to opt for setting, class size would be reduced and the expertise of the remedial specialists for the withdrawal of pupils would be made available where requested. The support services of the Resource Centre would facilitate the preparation of teaching materials for the new groupings. After lengthy discussion in various meetings all faculties, with the exception of Mathematics, were willing to accept mixed-ability groups for the new intake in September 1974. The Mathematics faculty wanted extra time for preparation. Under a new Head of Mathematics, the faculty set up a curriculum workshop and master classroom and adopted an individualised learning scheme of SMP workcards, backed up with a separate but related programme of tasks for homework and with this strategy they successfully introduced mixed-ability teaching in the following year. This development would have hardly been possible without the assistance of the Resource Centre. Subsequently mixed-ability groupings were extended into the Second Year, with the exception of French, and into the Third Year, with the exception of French and Mathematics and the one option (see Table 3.2 and Figure 3.5) where groups are governed by student choices. All faculties clarified their aims and all were required to devise assessment procedures for the new teaching situation. The assessment cards and systems of each faculty were examined and positively criticised in turn at the Heads of Faculty meetings. The changes were explained to the governing body and to the parents of the new intake. Several staff visited schools that had already developed mixed-ability teaching, and there was considerable expertise on the existing staff among teachers who had been teaching such classes in their previous schools and who had been involved in teaching in the 'teams' in the Humanities and in the subjects of Art, Technical and Home Economics where groups had been in mixed-ability for some years. From the subjective evaluation that has been made periodically within the school the balance of advantage seems to rest with mixed-ability. Furthermore, the Mathematics and Foreign Languages faculties definitely prefer setting across half-year groups to banding or streaming. In the Fourth and Fifth years there is a much more fluid situation, although at this stage many students are placed in target groups for O-level or CSE.

After a year of considerable changes the Headmaster was anxious that all the new developments should be successfully implemented and his watchword for the year was consolidation. One of my strategies at the time to foster deeper awareness of curriculum development and to lay a codified basis for co-operation and collaboration across the curriculum was to act as editor for the production of a staff curriculum handbook. The aims behind this adventure are shown in the original introduction.

Staff curriculum handbook

Introduction

There is already in existence a Staff Handbook outlining general school procedures and a Resource Centre Handbook which summarises the workings of the Resources Centre. This handbook, complementing the other two, will enable all colleagues to form a fairly comprehensive view of the work of the whole school. In particular, it aims:

1 to provide essential information relating to all aspects of the curriculum;
2 to inform all colleagues of the work of other Faculties and Departments;
3 to help all new staff and student teachers;

4 to promote curriculum development and encourage links and integration between Faculties and Departments and

5 to provide an ongoing record of the main policy decisions with regard to curriculum.

6 When the Middle Schools are established the curriculum of the two contributory schools ought to be similar and there must be some continuity between their curriculum and ours. Our needs and requirements will have to be stated and detailed discussions will have to take place with the Headmasters and the staff of the two Middle Schools.

This school is well advanced with curriculum development. The impetus to improve teaching materials, to create good learning environment, to update content with the development and expansion of knowledge, to establish new courses and amalgamate existing subjects, to co-operate across Faculty and Deparmental boundaries, to refine assessment procedures and to critically evaluate existing practices should be built into the organisation of the school and be part of our everyday thinking. This handbook has been produced to encourage such an ongoing dialogue between colleagues. Much work remains to be done. I have outlined some suggestions for further discussion (see shopping list). You will wish to add other items.

A further purpose was to clarify my relationships with colleagues who were Heads of Faculty and Department. A fairly comprehensive and demanding job specification was drawn up.

Role of the Head of Faculty and Department

The responsibilities of the Head of Faculty and Department are wide ranging. The size of the Faculty or the Department, the nature of the subject or discipline, the provision of specialist rooms and their distribution, the amount of time allocated on the time-table and other factors result in considerable variation.

The responsibilities have been arranged under the headings of Curriculum, Personnel and Resources and Organisation but obviously many of the categories overlap.

Curriculum

1 To construct flexible schemes of work for all years and to provide details of these in Faculty/Departmental syllabi and in the Curriculum Handbook of the school.

2 To provide a comprehensive range of courses leading to external examinations or internal assessment for all Fourth and Fifth years, and to liaise closely with Director of Studies for all Mode Three examinations.

3 To liaise closely with the Senior Mistress in all matters concerning internal and external examinations.

4 To integrate schemes of work with other Faculties and Departments and to co-operate in joint schemes of work where possible and desirable.

5 To keep assessment profiles for each pupil/student and to liaise closely with pastoral and careers staff in keeping central records up to date, and to provide regular assessment of all students whether by continuous assessment, tests or formal examinations.

6 To set homework, project and course work, and other individual programmes of work where necessary and desirable and where possible to offer extra-curriculum activities.

7 To be responsible for the grouping and organisation of teaching groups, and to inform, advise and counsel individuals when they select options for the Fourth and Fifth years and courses and subjects for the Sixth Form.

8 To liaise with Remedial Department where there are acute learning difficulties and where pupils/students are withdrawn for specialist help.

9 To be aware of curriculum projects and other developments in your subject area — new materials, approaches, techniques, equipment etc — and to disseminate these ideas among the Faculty. To evaluate periodically the work of the Faculty/Department.

10 To see that classes are given work when a member of the Faculty/Department is absent.

Personnel

11 To give support and encouragement to colleagues within your department and to promote their professional development. To liaise closely with Headmaster and Director of Studies on all matters of staffing, e.g. recommendations for upgrading, help with short-listing and interviewing candidates, drafting references for departmental members when they apply for new jobs etc.

12 To give particular help to staff in their induction year: observe and help in the classroom, guidance on work schemes and assessment procedures etc. To consult with Headmaster, County Adviser and Director of Studies throughout the probationary year about the progress of new staff.

13 To provide time-tables and outline schemes of work for students on teaching practice and to draft final student assessments; to liaise closely with Director of Studies and visiting tutors from College and Education Departments on all matters relating to teaching practice.

14 To hold regular Departmental/Faculty meetings. The minutes of these to be recorded and made available to the Headmaster and Director of Studies.
15 To foster team work and to promote the sharing of ideas, expertise and materials within the Faculty/Department.

Resources and Organisation

16 To be responsible for the requisitioning appropriate:
    (a) teaching and learning materials
    (b) material for the multi-media library in consultation with the Teacher-Librarian and Director of Studies
    (c) furniture, apparatus and equipment (FAE)
17 To work closely with the Resources Centre team in the production, indexing and storing of teaching and learning materials.
18 To help in programmes of in-service training that the Resource Centre provides and where possible promote independent in-service training programmes.
19 To see that rooms allocated to Faculty are kept presentable and made attractive by displays of teaching materials or pupils'/students' work; and to see that necessary safety precautions are taken.
20 To make forward plans for the deployment of staff and allocation of rooms for the timetable and to assist the Director of Studies in the time tabling of the Faculty/Department.
21 To attend, and contribute ideas at the Head of Faculty meeting, the main committee for discussing and, in many cases, determining the curriculum policy of the school.

    In brief the job of the Head of Faculty/Department is to organise, co-ordinate and inspire the work of the Faculty/Department.

Our major Heads of Faculty work at least 32 periods out of 40 in the teaching week and the Deputies work half a time-table. The teaching loads are heavy and the roles demanding. The paucity of time for curriculum development within a faculty and particularly across faculties within school time is manifestly obvious. In producing its section of the handbook, each faculty had to review critically its practices and commit to paper its policies. The handbook codified our practices, particularly the content of our courses.

Later that year at my request it was agreed that I become responsible for time-tabling. The Senior Mistress was willing to relinquish this task as she was shortly due to retire and as her examination responsibilities in the summer months had increased considerably. The arguments for consistent block time-tabling, particularly as analysed in the collection of papers edited by J. Walton, *The Secondary School Timetable*,[5] had impressed me. I knew the curriculum structure thoroughly and the teaching strengths of the staff and now that a faculty structure and core curriculum in the Fourth and Fifth Years, as well as the lower school, existed, it was an exciting challenge to put theory into operation. Blocking across half-year groups gives tremendous flexibility. It permits groupings to be easily altered, encourages team planning and evaluation and allows teachers to co-operate and support each other in the classroom. Although the school was not purpose-built as a comprehensive, every effort was made during that year to give every faculty a permanent base and a contiguous cluster of classrooms. Heads of Faculty are actively involved in the construction of the time-table. The Time-tabler devises a plan of the blocking arrangement making sure that there are no clashes which cannot be overcome and then faculties make decisions as to who takes which group in which room. The details of the blocking arrangement for the time-table for 1978–9 are given in Fig. 3.6. For explanations of the core and options in the Fourth Year refer to p. 73, while subjects in the option pools in the Sixth Form are only slightly modified to the scheme in Table 3.3.

In contrast to my criticism of the previous curricular structure and organisation of the school, I rated the work of the Resource Centre very highly. The rationale of resource-based learning, the organisation, the finance, the details about equipment, the indexing and retrieval systems are all well documented so I will keep my comments very brief. Thanks to the generous help of a very active Parent Teachers Association, offset litho and a coloured video-casette recorder have been installed in the last three years. The amount of ancillary help in the Centre has been increased to the equivalent of three full-time ancillaries. We now have four highly efficient and competent ancillary helpers, two of whom are kept busily engaged on typing, collating, indexing and storing teacher-produced material, while the other two ladies operate the reprographics room, the 'power-house' of the school, and record all radio and television programmes requested by the teaching staff. Quantitatively some 35,000 sheets of A4 pass through the duplicators in a typical week. The work of the Centre is indispensable to most Faculties and Departments and most Faculties spend more than one fifth of their total capitation on reprographic materials. Re-orders of existing materials now accounts for much of this finance, as most departments have well planned courses. The Centre still gives financial backing to new work. The in-service programme for all new teaching staff is continued but with some modifications and unfortunately a reduction in time. A general overview of the induction programme is given below.

	1 2	3 4	5 6	7 8
MON	4 *E.S. (B)* *Hum. (A)* CT/Sc	4 *E.S. (A)* *Hum. (B)* CT/Sc	U2 L3 *Ma. (A)* *P.E. (B)* CT/Sc	U2 L3 *Ma. (B)* *P.E. (A)* CT/Sc
TUES	4 *Ma. (B)* *Eng. (A)* E.S. (A) Hum. (B)	**Gen. Op.** *Ma. (A)* *Eng. (B)* E.S. (B) Hum. (A)	U3 L2 *Op. 2* Ma. (A) P.E. (B)	1 *Op. 1* Eng. (B) P.E. (A)
WEDS	U3 L2 *Ma. (B)* *Eng. (B)* Op. 1	U3 L2 *Ma. (B)* *Eng. (A)* Op. 2	4 *E.S. (A)* *Hum. (B)* Ma. (B) Eng. (A)	**6 games** *E.S. (B)* *Hum. (B)* Ma. (A) Eng. (B)
THUR	1 *CT/Sc* E.S. (B) Hum. (A)	1 *CT/Sc* E.S. (A) Hum. (B)	U2 L3 Ma. (B) P.E. (A)	**Gen. St.** *CT/Sc* Eng. (A) P.E. (B)
FRI	**Gen. Op.** *Op. 1* Ma. (A) — Eng. (B)	U2 L3 *Op. 2* Ma. (B) Eng. (A)	U3 L2 *Eng. (B)* *P.E. (A)* Op. 2	1 *Eng. (A)* *P.E. (B)* Op. 1

KEY: **6 Sixth** Sixth Form may be slightly altered.
5 Fifth
4 Fourth

Figure 3.6 *Blocking for time-table 1978–1979: arrangements for Fourth, Fifth and Sixth Years*

The Resource Centre and the preparation of teaching and learning materials

In-service training course

Some general points about the course:

1 It will last for three days; Friday, Monday and Tuesday.
2 Two members of staff will be released from teaching duties.
3 Pastoral duties will be taken as usual.
4 It is important that work is set for the classes that are covered by colleagues.
5 It is expected that staff going through the course will construct a unit of teaching material in consultation with their Head of Faculty/Department and with the Resource Centre team.

Objectives of the course:

1 To familiarise staff with the workings of the school's Resource Centre.
2 To examine teaching and learning materials produced in the school.
3 To examine methods of teaching and learning and to explore the importance of resources.
4 To show how such materials are produced and to give help with the production of new work.
5 To provide instruction in the use of audio-visual equipment.

Outline of course:

Friday

Period 1	Mrs Evans and Mrs Hammond	Instruction slip. Secretarial services. Type-script. Overheads. Open days.
Periods 2/3	Mrs Weaver and Mrs Yeomans	Reprographic machinery and capabilities. Radio and TV facilities. Overheads. Storage. Banda.
Period 4	Mr Abbs	Overview of curriculum development and Resource Centre work.
Periods 5/6	Mrs Sharratt	Library facilities – feature slip, classifying, indexing, storage, library use. Private study. Finances.
Period 7	Mr Yates	Photographic services.
Period 8	Mr Woolley	Audio-visual services. Use of overhead projectors. Practice with hardware.

Monday

Periods 1/2	Mrs Sharratt	Resources for teaching. Searching and ordering materials. Reviewing.

Periods 3/4	Mr Abbs	Curriculum planning of course and lessons, teaching and learning methods, preparation of resources.
Periods 5/6	Mrs Reynolds	Preparation of teaching materials.
Periods 7/8		Free to work on own materials.

Tuesday

| Period 1 | Mr Mincher | Design and lay-out of reprographic materials. |
| Period 2 onwards | | Free to work on own materials. |

The programme can be varied to meet the needs and requirements of staff on the course. If you have any special requests please see me in advance.

You are expected to produce teaching materials for your Faculty/Department in consultation with your Head of Faculty/Department. I would like to see the materials which you produce and to discuss them with you.

Please let us have any comment or criticism that you might have about the course or the workings of the Resource Centre. We are always looking for new ideas.

The most valued service is that of the reprographics unit and the school has a tradition of producing much of its own teaching material. An important aspect of the course, therefore, is to examine the rationale behind this 'cottage industry'.

The following extract gives some indication of our approach and the questions which we raise.

The planning and construction of printed teaching and learning material

Some general questions to ask yourself:

1 *Why produce your own material?* Some reasons:
   - (a) Because commercially produced material is expensive and becomes quickly outdated
   - (b) Because by writing your own material you can match the reading level of the material to that of the class
   - (c) Because your own material can be used more flexibly than a class text or a commercially produced pack of materials, much of which is often unsympathetic to your own caste of mind or the requirements of your own course
   - (e) Because locally produced material is cheaper. It is also easier to introduce new syllabi and curriculum innovations since there is no necessity to write off capital in the form of existing equipment and material

2 *What is the context?*
   (a) *Who*
       For whom is the material to be designated? What age range?
       What ability level? What knowledge in this field do the
       students already possess?
   (b) *What*
       What is the nature of the knowledge – scientific, mathe-
       matical, historical, moral, etc.?
       Within a subject, discipline or area of inquiry, what is the
       theme, topic or aspect?
   (c) *Purposes*
       What objectives or outcomes do you intend to achieve? Make
       these ends as clear and precise as possible. What CONCEPTS,
       IDEAS, FACTS, SKILLS, GENERALISATIONS, VALUES,
       ATTITUDES, etc. do you hope to get across or encourage in
       your students?
       Think 'deeply, systematically and reflectively' about what
       you are doing
   (d) *Why*
       What rationale or justification have you for holding these
       objectives?
   (e) *Method*
       Where do the teaching materials fit into the overall plan for
       this topic or theme?
       What methods of teaching or learning situation do you intend
       to use? How exactly are you going to use the printed materials?
   (f) *Content*
       What is the content to be and how are you going to arrange
       and present it? (see next section)
   (g) *Evaluation*
       How will you assess (i) whether your objectives have been
       achieved? (ii) the impact of your material?

3 *What is to be the content of the material?*
   (a) *Graphics*
       Presentation, lay-out, type of print, incorporation of illu-
       strations, etc.?
   (b) *Language*
       Appropriate level of vocabulary and syntax, need for repeti-
       tion and reinforcement, etc.?
   (c) *Variety*
       Use of drawings, diagrams, maps, cartoons, graphs, statistics,
       etc.?

(d) *Copyright*
Do you ignore? Ask permission? Re-write in your own words, etc.? It would seem intellectually honest at least to acknowledge

(e) *Sequence and structuring*
Is the format to be tightly structured or programmed, loosely structured, unstructured, of increasing difficulty or all of the same level, open ended or closed, etc.?

(f) *Activities and questions*
At end of unit, integral part of the text, separate student's work guide, etc.?

(g) *Overview*
Is a general guide to the materials necessary? Is a guide to other teachers who will or might use the unit necessary?

(h) *Initial questionnaire*
What do the students already know? What are their attitudes, values, beliefs, habits, etc.? This may be useful as a 'starter', stimulating interest. It could act as a check as to whether objectives are reached.

The resources organisation is essentially a team effort. There is a weekly meeting of the four ancillaries, the teacher-librarian and the teacher with responsibilities for audio-visual hardware and photography and myself, which deals mainly with routine administration and system maintenance. There have been various other types of resources committees with a broader base, drawing in teachers from the faculties, where resources, their construction and use, have been discussed in the context of the classroom. The Centre has also provided short in-service training sessions, on such topics as the use of overhead projectors, the construction and use of slide-tape sequence and photoplay, and the elements of graphical design. An example of what has been attempted is shown in Figure 3.7. In addition, the Centre produces handbooks, newspapers and advertising for the school, the Parent Teachers Association and to some extent the local community and offers its services to the local middle and first schools. An Open Day for visitors is held once a term.

Whereas in the Mitson era the Centre had a certain mystique and was spoken of with reverence in some quarters, the excellent facilities which it offers have now become normalised within the life of the school. The innovation has become fully institutionalised and most staff take its functioning for granted. It comes as a great shock to many when on interview or when taking up new posts they often find a very primitive state of resource provision and organisation in other schools. The economic recession and the educational 'back to basics' movement which has come in its wake, linked with the almost overpowering pressures

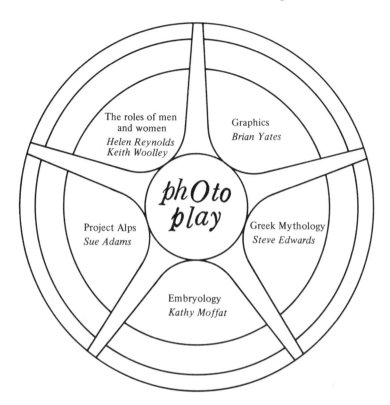

Original photographs, drawings, diagrams, documents, photographs, headings, epigrams or short written accounts, cartoons, graphs, charts etc., photographed and made into slides. Filmstrips cut up and converted to slides.

Music, discussion, live recordings, your commentary with single or several voices, recordings from radio, record or TV, songs, recordings, background effects etc., recorded on tape.

Photo-play: The combination of projected 'stills' and recorded sound.

Photo-play can be used in all areas of the curriculum to encourage worthwhile activities and interests. It is particularly suitable for promoting fictional and creative work, teaching practical skills and presenting documentary material. A programme can be used by the teacher for instruction, stimulus, enrichment, consolidation or revision.

Students and pupils can present their work in this format. A slide-tape sequence is perfectly acceptable for CSE project and course work. Oracy, visual and aesthetic education as well as literacy are thereby enhanced.

Commercial 'lists' can be bought and radiovision programmes recorded. The Resource Centre has the facilities and the know-how for the production of our own materials.

Distinct advantages occur where the teacher creates his own programme. He is in complete control of the content and the structuring of the photo-play; and after evaluation by pupils and teacher alterations can easily be made. The programme can be shown to a year group, single classes or small groups; and when stored in the multi-media library is made available to colleagues and individual students alike. It is a useful stepping stone to film making.

Figure 3.7 *Photoplay: Resource Centre in-service training*

exerted by the external examination system in a 13–18 high school have resulted in a more traditional use of resource material. Most of the resources constructed in the Centre are used to improve and back-up expository teaching. The work guide, booklet and question sheet replace or supplement the textbook, the overhead projector is often preferred for its versatility and cleanliness to the black board, and audio-visual resources are frequently integral parts of lessons. Traditional 'talk and chalk' is thus enormously enriched. Many teachers have created their own teaching materials, in some cases whole courses, and all the software: printed material including books, slides, video-tapes, audio-recordings, simulations, newspaper and magazine cuttings and other materials depending on the subject, are indexed in the library and are made readily available. The students have access to these resources for independent study when they are engaged upon inquiry, research or project work. However, these more individualised approaches to learning have not expanded to the extent that was once anticipated. The transmission model of imparting knowledge is the norm in most subjects and while the present public examinations have such a hold over the curriculum I doubt very much whether this situation will change. The innovatory potential of the Resource Centre has not yet been fully realised. Its contribution to improving traditional teaching styles and all aspects of communication within the school and the local community is highly valued by everyone. The work of the ancillary team is vital and a proper career structure and improved salary scale for this para-professional group is greatly needed. The resources team would like to see developed a national policy that provides every secondary school with a chartered librarian and gives teachers easy access to a multi-media resources officer.

Despite over a decade of curriculum reform, the external examinations system largely determines the curriculum in the upper part of the school. The parents, the governors and the local community want to see the school achieving good examination results and rightly so for, under the existing arrangements, academic qualifications are the means to higher education and prestigious careers and increasingly to all types of employment. Teachers are expected to deliver good results and faculties and departments come to be judged by their examination record. There is a definite pecking order. The A- and O-levels are the desired qualifications, the CSE and CEE are poor relations and Mode 3s are often judged to have even less merit. The examinations in most subjects apart from the up-dating of content remain remarkably similar to what they were before the establishment of the Schools Council. There are the same limiting constraints and the same emphasis on factual recall, quick response and speedy execution. How many aims are encapsulated in the present examination system? Very few, for most teachers. Even more harmful is the fact that the present system condemns most students to failure. While norm-referencing dominates the whole system there are built-in mechanisms for failure and it is impossible for most students to obtain O-levels. In the Fifth Year the school spends more money on fees for examination entries than on teaching and learning resources and at least one-third of the year is lost to teaching and taken over by examinations, 'mocks' and revision programmes. Inevitably students and teachers get very caught up in the system. The teachers are apt to transmit inert ideas and secondhand opinions, stick closely to the syllabus and anticipate likely questions while students swot up appropriate factual material which they hope to regurgitate in the examination. In brief and bluntly, the present examination system is not conducive to good teaching in many subjects. It is an axiom accepted by curriculum theorists that the curriculum comes first and assessment, including where appropriate examinations, is derived from the aims and objectives of the curriculum. Unless there are radical examination reforms at 16, the climate for curriculum development in the upper years of secondary education, particularly in suburban areas where demands for O-level success are especially strong, is not very favourable.

In addition to the faculty and resources committees and initiatives the other formal avenue for curriculum development inside the school is the working party. Over the past three years the main working parties dealing with curricular questions have been concerned with remedial provision and organisation, the Bullock Report and Mathematics across the curriculum. Also over the last three years all faculties have attended area curriculum meetings with colleagues from first and middle schools to prepare for three-tier organisation. As these have not been specifically school-based I will not provide details. The principle of continuity, as applied to curricular structures and the development of knowledge, concepts, skills and attitudes, cannot be overemphasised and is sufficient reason why curriculum development cannot be restricted to the confines of one school.

The Bullock Report I would regard as perhaps the most important document of recent times pertinent to curriculum development. Discussions on this report began at a staff meeting. All the staff were circulated with the principal and some of the minor recommendations and a list of questions for discussion. The booklet which was finally produced had this short introduction and list of contents.

Introduction to the working party report: language across the curriculum

'Learning to Communicate is at the heart of education'
'Educational failure is largely linguistic failure'

After the initial examination of the contents of the Bullock Report at two staff meetings at the end of the autumn term 1975, a working party was set up to explore further some of the issues raised by this important inquiry and to outline a policy for Codsall School for language across the curriculum.

The members of the working party were: Mr Bryans (Social Science), Mrs Cunnington (Foreign Languages), Mrs Frost (Mathematics), Mr Job and Mr Jurkiewicz (Sciences), Mrs Larkham (Business Studies and Careers), Mr Platt (Creative Technology), Mrs Reynolds (Social Sciences), Mrs Sharratt (Teacher-Librarian) and Mrs Vanstone and Miss Watson (English). Mr Abbs (Director of Studies) chaired the meetings and drafted the report. Other colleagues attended specific meetings. The group met regularly during Thursday lunch times during the spring and summer terms of 1976.

If the report is to be effective all colleagues should carefully study the recommendations.

After discussions at various levels at Departmental, Faculty and Staff meetings, the recommendations, modified where this is thought to be desirable, can be implemented by all teachers at this school. It is just as important that we regularly reflect on our present classroom practices and critically scrutinise all aspects of our use of language when teaching. If this is to be more than a pious aspiration we must plan further occasions to examine in depth the ways in which we as teachers use language. The Bullock Report must be a beginning to a continuing dialogue between teachers and between teachers and students about the importance, structure and functions of language. Books can be read and conferences attended (the Open University runs courses on Language and Learning and on Reading Development) but the working party recommended above all that aspects of the use of language be regular items on the agendas of Faculty, Departmental and Heads of Faculty meetings. For instance, samples of written work, tape recorded lessons on group work, marking schemes, work sheets, supporting books and other reading material could be reviewed and experiences exchanged.

Such workshop sessions are essential if we are to gain a greater understanding into the workings of language.

A main aim of this report is to sensitise teachers to the crucial role that language plays in learning. With greater awareness about the intricacies of language development in our students we should as teachers make more effective use of language in our teaching and hence further the learning of our students.

Contents of working party report on Bullock
Working party report: language across the curriculum

1 Introduction   1
2 Oracy: oral and aural work in the curriculum   2-3
3 Writing across the curriculum   4-5
4 Reading across the curriculum   6
5 Marking scheme: policy for all teachers   7
6 Multi-media library   8-9
7 Resource Centre facilities: problems and some
    possible solutions   10
8 Remedial provisions   11
9 Study skills   12

Appendices

1 Principal recommendations of the Bullock Report   13-14
2 Techniques of Study   (Separate booklet)
3 Techniques of Study: Fourth and Fifth year   (Separate booklet)
4 Reading List   15

These extracts provide a simple overview of the organisation and intentions of the working party. The members of the working party exchanged views and practices with their faculty colleagues on the various issues as they arose. After the report was compiled and distributed a plenary session was held at a special staff meeting. Subsequently aspects of the report have been regularly placed on the agenda of faculty meetings.

In contrast, the work on Mathematics across the curriculum largely consisted of practical sessions. The school teaches modern Mathematics but teachers who use Mathematics in other subject areas were often using different techniques and strategies, for instance, in handling fractions, percentages and formulae, to those used by the Mathematics faculty. Obviously this situation confused many students. The Mathematics faculty outlined the philosophy of modern Mathematics, showed how they handled number and measurement and how they taught various aspects of their curriculum. Staff from other faculties introduced problems they experienced with students and a most useful and fruitful exchange of views took place. It is to be hoped that all teachers who use mathematics will now adopt similar techniques and strategies.

I have only outlined those aspects of curriculum development which concern all or most staff. Most curriculum development takes place within the confines of a faculty or department. Comprehensive reorganisation, the establishment of a Resource Centre and in-service courses, restructuring to a faculty system, mixed-ability teaching, the compiling of a curriculum handbook, and three-tier reorganisation have successively stimulated each department to review and modify its curricular policies and practices. All faculties cater for the whole ability range and have devised examination courses for all students. The school has developed over a dozen Mode 3 examinations at CSE. All faculties have now held an Open Evening for parents to explain and demonstrate their work. It would be invidious here to draw special attention to the work and initiatives of any one faculty.

A sound organisation, good channels of communication, the support of an efficient Resource Centre, time-tabling which encourages rather than frustrates staff collaboration, and curriculum and staff handbooks facilitate curriculum development and sound practice but they do not guarantee it. I have written mainly about structural supports of one kind or another, all of which are of vital importance. I also meet each Head of Faculty and Department individually several times during the year to discuss time-tabling, forward planning, resources, student teachers, teachers in their induction year, Mode 3 examinations and other matters that arise. At these times I often attempt to raise other and wider curricular issues. Much talk about curriculum and preparation of work is carried out informally. Many teachers at Codsall put hours of extra effort into producing resources. In large organisations it would be foolish indeed to rely on informal channels and teacher goodwill, highly desirable though both are, to sustain curriculum development. At the heart of curriculum development is the relationship between a teacher and student, teacher and small group and teacher and class. The key figure is the teacher. He must know what he is doing and why, be an expert in his subject area, understand his students, their personalities, backgrounds, aspirations, fears, interests and abilities, know how to get his students on the inside of his subject and develop their understanding and skills, foster inquiring attitudes and know how to assess his students' learning and to evaluate his own practices. It is a highly complex business. In being complex it requires time — time for reflection, time for study, time for observations of colleagues at work, time for clarifying aims and objectives and evaluating methods, content and progress in the light of these aims, and time for reviewing existing resources and where necessary constructing new ones. Knowledge, technology and society do not stand still. In the educational field alone there is such a phenomenal growth in the literature and research that even the professionals in the curricular business have difficulties in keeping up with their reading. Indeed, as stated earlier, there is an enormous theoretical gap between most teachers and academic educationalists and professional curriculum developers. If curriculum development in the school is to be purposeful and well-informed and to become firmly rooted, teachers must be given the time and support to catch up with current development and to critically examine their own practices.

Time for school-based curriculum development must be built into the annual programme of the school. Nearly all the various meetings that I have referred to have taken place in the late afternoon after school or in the lunch break, when teachers are often tired and weighed down by more immediate pressures, not least classes to prepare for and work to assess. Even with block time-tabling a member of a faculty will often be teaching Sixth-formers, whose time-table cuts across the blocks, so it is very rare for all members of a faculty to be available for a meeting at the same time. There is also the permanent problem of providing 'cover' for teachers who are absent. Unless class sizes are going to be appreciably increased or classes be left with work and substitute teachers, both of which are highly undesirable practices, the feasibility of in-service training in school time is severely limited. When sessions and programmes of in-service training are held after school hours there is a tendency for only the committed and converted to attend. When teachers attend courses elsewhere and report back to colleagues, immediacy and relevance are often lacking and the consequences for the school usually negligible unless the teacher is a very forceful and determined character. Even then, time to influence colleagues and persuade committees is required. In our discussions at Codsall over mixed-ability teaching, general curricular aims, resource creation, pupil assessment, Language and Mathematics across the curriculum, to mention some of the more important issues, many of us are aware that analysis is often not sufficiently detailed, and that staff are not given enough time to reflect and think through the implications of any proposed changes. There is the constant danger that once a policy has been committed to paper and decisions taken the issue is finished with. Agreed policy and clear decisions are essential first steps. Decisions about what takes place in the classroom cannot be wrapped neatly into packages and filed away. Most teachers are very cynical about paper 'bumpf', especially that which comes from any hierarchical source. They deserve civilised conditions in which they can examine critically existing practices and explore the rationale and implications of any proposed new development or innovation. These reviews and discussions should take place regularly, and systematically focus on all aspects of school life.

A national policy for school-based in-service training and curriculum development is wanted. One or two weeks a year where all the staff meet without the students or a four-day week for students and a five-day

week for staff are possibilities. If the school is to be the unit of accountability, if teachers are to have real professional responsibilities and if
parents, the local community and students, as recommended by the
Taylor Report, are going to be significantly involved, or in other words
if school-based curriculum development is to become firmly and effectively rooted in our schools, a structured programme of in-service training with ample time must be created for all schools. Teachers in the
day-to-day working context of their own school, each with its unique
history and social and environmental conditions, require additional time
to work out their curricular policies, discuss their implementation and
improvement, and evaluate to what extent students are learning what
they are supposed to be learning. Outside advice and constructive criticism from advisers, theorists, researchers, parents, students and community representatives should be an integral part of the programme, as
should visits to other educational institutions and observation of different styles and ways of learning.

Notes

1 N. Beswick, *School Resource Centres*, Schools Council Working
   Paper 43, London, Evans/Methuen, 1972.
2 N. Beswick, *Organizing Resources*, London, Heinemann, 1975.
3 J. White, *Towards a Compulsory Curriculum*, London, Routledge &
   Kegan Paul, 1973.
4 Department of Education and Science, *Education in Schools: A
   Consultative Document* (Green Paper), London: HMSO, 1977.
5 J. Walton (ed.), *The Secondary School Timetable*, London, Ward
   Lock, 1972.
6 See Beswick 1972, op. cit.; 1975, op. cit.; and *Resource Based Learning*, London: Heinemann, 1977; M. Holder and E. Hewton, 'A school
   resource centre', *British Journal of Educational Technology*, vol. 4,
   January 1973, p. 1; M. Holder and R. Mitson, *Resource Centres*,
   London, Methuen, 1974; R. Mitson, 'A view of resource centres',
   Ideas, no. 22, June 1973.

Chapter 4

Curriculum development and staff development at the Abraham Moss Centre

Ron Mitson

If teaching is not a science with agreed techniques, it involves at least a range of skills that can be practised and become perfected in action. Teachers develop a certain adequacy of curriculum organisation and exposition, questioning, and other classroom skills that can eventually become almost second nature to them. Such skills will not be modified, or extended, or reappraised, merely by exposure to alternatives at the level of theory. In many cases the conditioning is so deep that only the opportunity to develop adequacy in the practice of an alternative or new skill will enable the teacher to feel secure enough to adopt that new skill. New teachers entering the profession are likely to have been introduced on their Certificate and Post-graduate courses to the possibility of the use of a wider range of skills in addition to the expository approach. However, by the time they enter the profession and feel the strain of responsibility for their first class, they have been conditioned themselves as pupils for at least fifteen years in education to a view of teaching as being based on the expository method with the teacher as the central and often only resource. Finding themselves surrounded by colleagues who rely almost entirely on that method, they too are likely to place their reliance almost completely on it, secure in the feeling built almost into the marrow of their bones that it 'is' teaching. Certainly, many experienced teachers will attend in-service courses, return to the school expressing an interest, possibly even an enthusiasm, and yet the course will prove to have minimal influence upon their own approach. Few are likely to be foolish enough to desert one form of practice in which they are already proficient for another in which they have had no chance to explore their adequacy outside the classroom and may therefore fail.

The most successful practice is undoubtedly school-based and collaborative, and encompasses both the necessary in-service training and the provision of all the support services required. When staff are involved as team members working together, they have the ideal environment for professional support and development. As a team, they can plan together, pool ideas, share the development of materials, work out the organisation of the classroom, be briefed by the members who have prepared the work, work together and support each other in the classroom and carry out an honest professional reappraisal of the work and organisation afterwards. Both the material and approach gain from the pooling and cross-fertilisation of ideas and the benefits of learning from each other in action are enormous, and lead to a professional satisfaction, motivation and maturity that the individual teacher working in isolation can never achieve. Aware that they are honestly understanding and sharing the burden and that the staffroom façade is no longer essential, they lose their insularity and defensiveness and staffroom conversations and staff meetings become less superficial. Such circumstances diminish the possibility of the somewhat introverted self-critical teacher who never really sees others at work, going home each day feeling that he has not lived up to the occasion, and the somewhat extroverted unselfcritical teacher living continuously under the delusion that his performance cannot be improved. All learn from each other and support each other at the level of practice.

Regular team meetings are an essential part of this, and everything possible must be done to ensure that each team has a meeting time included on the time-table. Where possible, an extra member should be allocated to the team, allowing the flexible sharing of non-teaching periods. In this way, team cover can usually be an internal matter and a member of the team may be released by agreement to produce materials or attend a particular school-based in-service training course.

Where it is essential that staff adopt particular teaching approaches, it is helpful if induction courses can be laid on before the beginning of the new school year to give new staff, not just probationers, some indication of both the methods employed and the services available to them. Obviously attendance under present circumstances is entirely voluntary, but a short two- or three-day course can engage a high percentage of attendance.

At the Abraham Moss Centre we have a number of reasons for developing in-service training and school-based curriculum development. The Centre includes a number of open-plan areas, in which teachers cannot operate as they operate in an ordinary classroom and still be effective. Two teachers working with a large group cannot divide it into two separate groups and teach in the traditional expository fashion without each group of pupils being distracted by the other teacher and the two teachers having to compete for attention.

Because the Centre is a community centre, we have to support our staff in adapting to work in it. In many cases, in fact, we have to face the problem of teachers who come imbued with the ideals of community but who have been so hemmed in by the pressures of coping in the classroom alone that they have not been able to involve themselves as much as they would like in, and expand their view of, the community. Table 4.1 is an example of a community in-service training programme.

Comprehensive education, if it stems from a philosophy of valuing all equally and of equality of opportunity, must imply mixed-ability teaching, certainly during the early years. Of course, access to options at different levels of understanding, preceded by full advice, and no rejection of the pupil's final choice may replace this in the Fourth and Fifth Years.

Mixed-ability teaching will only be effective if a major change takes place in teaching approach. The traditional mainly expository teaching approach is effective only with groups of pupils of homogeneous ability who can work more or less at the same speed. If the same approach is used with groups which include the whole ability range, the work will be too fast for some and too slow for others, unless the learning opportunities are closely structured. Even creating groups of different levels of ability within the class, and dealing with each group in turn will not provide the answer. The teacher will not be able to initiate the work of, and deal with the problems of, each separate group without leaving other groups waiting for the next instructions or help.

In order to overcome this we structure basic course material very simply and clearly so that when pupils enter the classroom they can begin work straightaway from the point at which they left off and can work very much at their own pace. At the beginning of each structured work unit there is a note to the teacher indicating what the aims and target group of the unit are, and a guide to the pupil telling him how to make use of the unit. Normally, units are structured at an average level and an easier level of understanding. The average-level unit leads out to options of greater difficulty, which will stretch the brightest pupils. The easier-level unit is supported by talking-page and taped units for those pupils who find reading very difficult although, given that the brighter pupils are more capable of continued self-sufficiency in this approach, the teacher is freed to devote more of his time to those, such as the slow readers, who need it most. At the same time, the brightest pupils are not held back waiting for the rest, but are supplied with additional more difficult material that they can work, and extend themselves, on.

Figure 4.1 is an example of a structured unit used in the 2nd year.

I believe it to be important that we distinguish between independent learning and individualised learning. We are concerned to train our pupils in the skills of learning and using resources, and to help them to learn gradually, by working within a closely structured framework, how to

TABLE 4.1 *A community in-service training*

AMC In-service training course: getting to know Cheetham and Crumpsall (8–9 February 1978)

Course outline

DAY 1

Time	Topic	Details	Group leader	Other personnel	Meeting place
9.00–9.30	General introduction	Handouts, explanations, questions from course members, etc.	Tom Thompson		A4
	The area physically				
9.30–11.00	Cheetham present	A general look at the area on foot and by minibus with an opportunity to see some of the current focal points and to discuss informally with the local Community Development Officer	Chris Ensor (Community Development Officer)	Glynis Francis (Youth and Community Neighbourhood Worker)	Depart from A4
11.00–11.15	Coffee				A19
11.15–1.15	Cheetham past	A look at Cheetham as it used to be through the eyes of someone who has lived and worked in the area	Chris Ensor	Izzy Wallman (Librarian – AMC Library)	A19
	Cheetham future	A planner outlines future developments for the area		Gas Hill (Manchester Planning Department)	
1.15–2.00	Lunch	Taken in Dining 1 cafeteria style but with a table reserved for the group		Course members Glynis Francis and anyone else who can make it	Dining 1

Time	Topic	Details	Group leader	Other personnel	Meeting place
	The area socially				
2.00–4.00	Pre-school needs	Visit the Cheetham Childminders Research Centre (MCCR). An opportunity to investigate pre-school provision in the district and to see the playbus	Glynis Francis	Mary Duncan (Childminders' Centre) Angela Kelly (Playbus)	301 Cheetham Hill Road
4.00–4.30	Tea				A11
4.30–6.00	Youth initiatives	Workers involved in a variety of non-club-based youth projects explain their objectives and discuss youth work in this area	Glynis Francis	Margaret Kenny-Levick, John Wood (Cheetham coffee bar project), Stephen McIntyre (Cheetham adventure playground), Kathleen Sayer, Sheena Melrose (Residential wing AMC)	A11
6.00–7.30	Meal	80p paid at the time please		Course members and anyone else who can make it	Bookable dining room AMC
7.30–9.00	Youth clubs	Introduction to club-based work. Visits to two clubs in the area	Dick Chamberlain (Youth Tutor AMC) Fr Paul Jones (St. Chads YC)	Dick Chamberlain	Youth club office AM
9.00–		Discussion over a pint			By arrangement

DAY 2

The area socially

Time	Topic	Description	Presenter	People	Room
9.30–11.00	Ethnic minorities	A structured discussion with workers in that area	Hartley Hanley (MCCR)	Tutu Eko (Advice Worker), Sid Jaspar, Ruhi Shah, Irving Smith	A19
11.00–11.15	Coffee				Coffee
11.15–1.00	Handicapped children	The problem of coping with various degrees of handicap and a look at some local developments	Margaret Evans (Community Development Officer)	Some parents of handicapped children	A19
1.00–2.00	Lunch	As for day 1			
2.00–4.00	Community development initiatives	A look at community work in the area with some local workers	Chris Ensor	Alice Kirkham, Betty Rosenbloom (Cheetham Community Association) Lesley Willey, Lesley Willey, Pat Ogle, Sheila Saunders, Tudor Owen (Advice Project), Glynis Francis	Cheetham Library basement
4.00–4.30	Tea and post-mortem	A chance to evaluate the course	Tom Thompson		A11

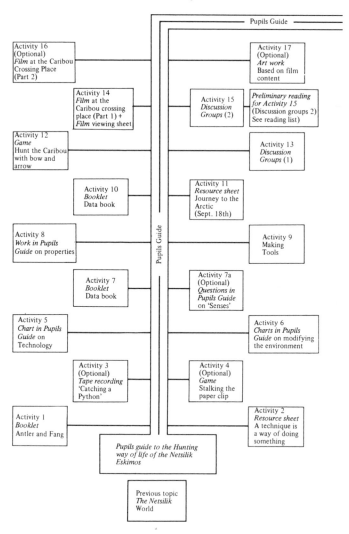

Figure 4.1 *A community in-service training programme*

One advantage of this programme is that it is both heavily structured and yet very flexible. It is aimed at average and above average students (there is also a parallel level for less able students) and is graded so that the work becomes progressively harder as the pupil works through it. He is able to cope with increasingly difficult work because it has been preceded by carefully structured work guiding him through the topic step by step.

103

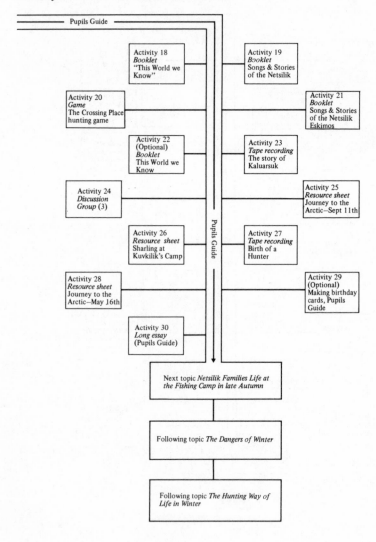

The programme is designed to last a month but could be 'tailored' to suit individuals. Although a large group of pupils might all be working on this unit, a teacher could indicate on each pupil's work programme exactly which 'activities' that pupil would be best occupied in doing. These individual 'routes' through the work might all be different and yet appropriate to each pupil.

organise the development of their own learning and become more independent in learning. The units may include some choices of options, but they are not individualised in the sense of providing a completely separate programme of study to suit the individual interests and inclinations of each pupil. The impossibility of one teacher creating such a range is obvious. The danger in not attempting it is that, at an age when pupils need a secure and supportive framework in which to work, they may be left in the insecure and uncertain vacuum created by the teacher providing — because of lack of time — verbal guidance that is too vague, restricted, and lacking in direction. This lack of direction is often equated with 'progressive' education, and certainly control and direction are much more difficult to achieve if the individual needs of pupils in terms of pace of work are catered for, and extremely difficult to achieve if individual interest is given priority. The combination of individual pace of work and direction, depending as it does on structured work that obviates over-dependence on the teacher, is nevertheless worth every effort to achieve.

We hope to develop independence in learning even further with fifteen- and sixteen-year-olds. Young people, who can feel their budding adulthood, are often asked to show a more adult and responsible approach to their work but demeaned by being left in a position where they have no idea what to do next until the teacher walks into the classroom and says, 'Now, today we are going to do so-and-so'. Those with an academic motivation and goal which they feel the school may still fulfil will usually accept all this unconsciously as an inevitable part of the system, and suffer uncomplainingly. The ceaseless search for the 'interesting' and 'relevant' course for those without academic motivation may never succeed. (The pretence that all work is interesting may in any case be somewhat hollow.) For them, the 'feel' of work itself may be more relevant, and they may gain far more incentive and motivation from not being left in the completely dependent situation with no idea what work they are expected to do from one hour to the next, but from being placed in a position where they will be able to adopt a comparatively adult approach to their work, and have some control over their own destinies in being able, to an increasing extent, to organise the development of their own learning.

Our final aim is a community one of producing adults who will be capable of continued learning throughout life in a society which now stresses the importance of that. The achievement of such a goal will depend on people gradually acquiring that capacity by undergoing the experience themselves, through practice rather than exhortation. Apparent developments in education are sometimes not reflected in what is happening in schools and classrooms throughout the system. It is on occasions as if the more things change, the more they remain the same.

105

Ideas and movements that emerge at the macro-level sometimes make very little impact because they do not penetrate effectively to the micro-level. Mixed-ability teaching, and adult learning throughout life, may be two examples of this. For the former, unless there is a significant change in what happens between the teacher and the pupil in the classroom, at the micro-level, the approach can be claimed to be ineffective, and denigrated at the macro-level, although its influence has not really been fully developed and tested. The latter is an example of something that can be accepted as happening and that many pay lip-service to, when no fundamental change has taken place at all.

As a further major step towards that final aim, we hope to create for our fifteen- and sixteen-year-olds a year's self-contained courses in particular subjects which at the beginning of the year indicate to the pupil:

(i) the information he has to make his by the end of the year

(ii) the ideas he has to understand, and use in his thinking, and relate to that information

(iii) the skills he has to practise and become proficient in, linked to a range of skill-building packs, so that, when the student has to lead or join in a discussion group, carry out an interview, or provide a statistical analysis, he will be able as an individual to improve his competence in the activity by consulting the appropriate skill-building unit at that level

(iv) a series of areas of further reading and study and research related to the development of the course.

All this will be arranged around a series of sessions with the teacher throughout the year, the number of those sessions depending on the nature of the subject and the extent of laboratory work or oral training required. The teacher will otherwise always be available, acting in the capacity of tutor, making regular checks on the progress of each student week by week and helping out where problems arise.

It is to ensure that developments such as this can eventually penetrate to and take place at the micro-level that school-based in-service training is absolutely essential. The dissemination of ideas can take place on courses outside the school, in teachers' centres, or in school, but the major element of in-service training within the school itself, although obviously not all of it, must be concerned with increasing the effectiveness of what the school is trying to do. It is at this stage that the broader elements of secondary education theory and practice should be related to the particular needs of the school, its curriculum, its teachers and its pupils. It is in its recognition of this, and in its relevance to actual practice within the classroom, that the major justification for school-based in-service training exists.

Throughout the year we organise a programme of in-service training (see Figure 4.2), and try to release staff for as much as a week at a time

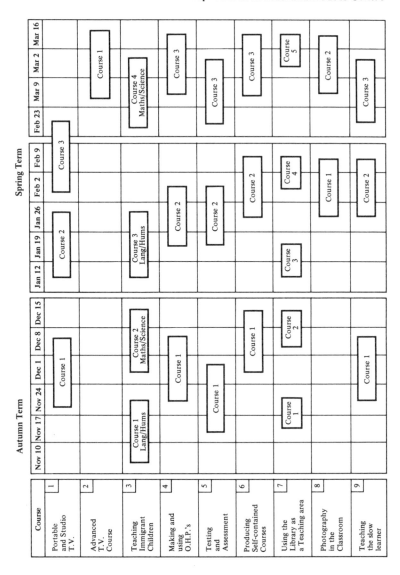

	1	2	3	4	5
Course Title	Portable and Studio T.V.	Advanced T.V.	Teaching Immigrant Students	Making and using O.H.P.'s	Testing and Assessment
Course Tutor	Helen Clay	Sidney Kenny-Levick	Abul Maula	Donald Hough	David Watchorn
Details of the Course (Note: Course No. 5 on testing and assessment takes place on Tuesdays. i.e. 1) Nov. 15, 22, 29th. 2) Jan. 17, 24, 31st. 3) Feb. 21, 28th. 4) April 11, 18, 25th. 5) June 20, 27th. July 4th.	A course for those who know little or nothing about the use of T.V. in education. The course will concentrate on the basics of T.V. production and will be designed so that short T.V. programmes can be made, using both the portable and studio cameras. Contact Helen Clay on Ext. 224.	The advanced course is available to those who already have some experience of using T.V. equipment. Advanced studio techniques such as using and mixing three cameras, dubbing sound and editing tape will all be covered. Contact Sidney Kenny-Levick on Ext. 234.	This course is in two parts. Courses 2, 4 and 6 are for Maths and Science teachers. Courses 1, 3 and 5 are for teachers of other subjects. The aim of these courses is to point out the difficulties immigrant students have due to language and cultural background and help staff to overcome these difficulties, particularly when producing teaching material. Contact Abul Maula on Ext. 226.	A practical course where staff can learn about making permanent O.H.P.'s, adding colour, making overlays and other ways of using overhead projections. The course will also cover the use of the overhead projector in the classroom. Contact Donald Hough on Ext. 233,	This is a practical course designed to help staff prepare a variety of tests and evaluate the results. It will also cover various methods of examination preparation which students can be offered. Contact David Watchorn on Ext. 226.

Summer Term

No.	Course
1	Portable and Studio T.V.
2	Advanced Immigrant Students
3	Teaching Immigrant Students
4	Making and using O.H.P.'s
5	Testing and Assessment
6	Producing Self-contained Courses
7	Using the Library as a Teaching area
8	Photography in the Classroom
9	Teaching the slow learner

Schedule (weeks commencing Apr 13, Apr 20, Apr 27, May 4, May 11, May 18, May 25, Jun 8, Jun 15, Jun 22, Jun 29, Jul 6, Jul 13, Jul 20):

Course	Scheduled sessions
1. Portable and Studio T.V.	Course 4 (Apr 13–Apr 20); Course 5 (May 11–May 25)
2. Advanced Immigrant Students	Course 5 Lang/Hums (Apr 27–May 4); Course 2 (Jun 8–Jun 15); Course 3 (Jul 6–Jul 13)
3. Teaching Immigrant Students	Course 4 (Apr 27–May 4); Course 6 Maths/Science (Jun 15–Jun 29)
4. Making and using O.H.P.'s	Course 4 (Apr 13–Apr 20); Course 4 (Apr 27); Course 5 (Jun 8–Jun 22)
5. Testing and Assessment	Course 5 (May 11–May 25); Course 5 (Jun 22–Jul 6)
6. Producing Self-contained Courses	Course 6 (Apr 27–May 4); Course 6 (Jun 22–Jul 6)
7. Using the Library as a Teaching area	Course 6 (May 4); Course 3 (Apr 27–May 11); Course 7 (Jun 8–Jun 15); Course 8 (Jul 13–Jul 20)
8. Photography in the Classroom	Course 4 (Apr 27–May 11); Course 4 (Jun 8–Jun 22)
9. Teaching the slow learner	Course 4 (Apr 13–Apr 20); Course 5 (Jun 15–Jun 29)

Course Title	Producing Self-contained Courses	Using the Library as a Teaching Area	Photography in the Classroom	Teaching the Slow Learner
	6	7	8	9
Course Tutor	Rod Hill	Irene Thompson	To be announced	Ann Portus and Bernard Slattery
Details of the course	The aim of this course is to demonstrate the procedure for producing a self-contained course. It will also look at course content such as 'unit production' and also offer suggestions on the ways in which courses can be structured. Contact Rod Hill on Ext. 252.	The emphasis in this course will be on: a) showing the ways in which the library can be used. b) using guided work programmes in the library. c) showing what support services the libary staff can offer. Contact Irene Thompson on Ext. 261.	This couse will cover three main areas: a) How to take photographs and slides for classroom use. b) How to make and use tape/slide sequences. c) Using photographs and slides as part of work programmes. Contact Helen Clay (224) Rod Hill (252)	This course is divided into two parts. Bernard Slattery will concentrate on producing material and organising learning situations for slow learners. Ann Portus will look at the reading problems experienced by slow learners and show how booklets and other printed material can be made more 'readable' for this group. Contact both on Ext. 226.

Figure 4.2

110

from time-table so that they may attend the workshops and courses. We are able to do this not because we have additional staff but because so far our staff have accepted the situation on the basis that if they cover for other staff on courses, other staff will cover for them, and the professional benefits are therefore reciprocal. There is, of course, additional provision in the evenings and on Saturday mornings which many staff will give up their own time to take advantage of.

Although we do arrange the occasional conference and discussion on aims, and the curriculum, most of the internal courses are organised so that staff may learn at the practical level from other colleagues who have already developed an expertise in a particular field, and our own staff who have developed particular skills are used as valuable resources. Wherever possible, the courses are organised so that staff may explore the idea at the level of experience rather than just at the level of theory, so that, by having-a-go in practice, they may develop the adequacy to make them feel secure enough to introduce the skill into the classroom. Often, the support of working with a team, itself one of the most effective forms of in-service training, has already carried them to the point of attempting the skill, and the experience in the course is helping them to develop it.

Courses offered in the programme, in addition to the community course already dealt with, include:

1 The design and structuring of learning materials so that they may be used by the teacher and pupil, or the pupil independently
2 The development of course guides that link teacher-produced and commercial resources into integrated work units
3 The production of such audio-visual resources as overhead projector transparencies and tape/slide links
4 Classroom management, related to working in open-plan environments and using role play as a technique in the course itself. A variety of aspects are dealt with, such as that when two teachers are working together in one room, there is a tendency for each to expect the other to set the standard of behaviour and noise level, and therefore for the situation to be less well controlled initially than it might be.

We ask all staff involved in in-service training courses to complete an evaluation sheet on the course after they have finished so that we have regular feedback on how the courses may be improved (see Table 4.2).

It is important that a school developing its own school-based in-service training should not be too inbred, and essential that links with teachers' centres, the Local Authority and national provision should be maintained and made full use of so that the wider thinking about education philosophy, theory and practice continues alongside the concentration on

TABLE 4.2 *In-service evaluation sheet – induction course*

Name _____ Date _____

Day, session and time	Comments and suggestions
Monday 9.15–10.45 Introduction to Centre Services (R. Hill & J. Dyson)	
Monday 11.00–12.15 Layout and presentation of material (D. Hough)	
Monday 1.15–3.15 Making teaching material	
Tuesday 9.15–10.00 The Centre Library	
Tuesday 10.00–10.45 The Library as a teaching/ learning area (R. Hill)	
Tuesday 11.00–12.15 and 1.15–3.15 Making a guided work programme for use in the library	
Wednesday 9.15–12.15 Meeting the needs of slow learners (B. Slattery)	
Wednesday 1.15–3.15 Introduction to the Centre T.V. Service (K. Fingleton)	

Thursday
9.15–12.15
Choosing and using the
Media
(K. Fingleton)

Thursday
1.15–3.15
The T.V. Studio
(K. Fingleton)

Friday
9.15–12.15
The structuring of teaching
material
(R. Hill)

Friday
1.15–2.15
The Centre's
Photographic Services
(R. McCulloch)

Friday
2.15–3.15
In-Service Training/
learning techniques and
the Centre
(R. Mitson)

General Comments

the practical implementation of ideas that school-based in-service training lends itself to. For that reason, attendance at courses outside the Centre is normally approved only when staff will agree to provide a written report and report back to and discuss the courses with all those who may be interested.

An in-service programme needs effective support services and we place some priority on technical support at the audio-visual level. Such services are centralised, and technicians' help in setting up equipment is often available to staff. Where staff are developing or using skills in producing resources, we think it important that these resources should not appear third-rate in comparison with any produced in the world outside school, and by association make school appear third-rate. For that reason, secretarial and reprographic services are provided to support staff in their production of materials.

All in-service training is organised by a director of staff support services who is an appointment at deputy level. He works through, and

113

gains feedback and ideas from, a committee, ensuring that other staff are involved in the thinking and planning.

The whole range of activity of school-based curriculum development and in-service training is professionally absolutely essential and beneficial and yet a strain on the normal teaching day. We need to explore all kinds of ways of making such provision effective. One wonders, for instance, about the possibility of greater involvement of final year students in teams such as ours in order to release an experienced team member, who may then have the benefit of in-service training without at the same time being conscious of the burden he is placing on his colleagues. I doubt whether we shall ever be able really to consider ourselves a profession as long as the extent of our own day at school coincides with that of the pupils, and time for all the very essential professional aspects of discussing, planning, preparing, reappraising, developing new skills has to be snatched when it can be from the holes and corners of the hectic school day, or depend upon the goodwill of colleagues outside that day. In a world that is changing so rapidly, socially and technologically, ongoing school-based curriculum development and in-service training becomes more and more essential. It should be built in as a mandatory part of the professional scene, not left to chance.

Even if one reached that stage, however, the situation would still be fraught with difficulties. Our own efforts at school-based curriculum development have been valuable. The development of Core Studies by our first Curriculum Consultative Committee captured the imagination of the majority of staff and filled the school with a professional concern and commitment unrivalled by any institution. Despite the momentum created by this, putting the ideas into practice proved to be an enormous burden for the members of a single school's staff to shoulder. Eventually the demands of those studies outside the Cores had to be fulfilled also, work on some of the more exciting developments had to be shelved, and the frustration of not being able to continue the work bit deep. The self-contained courses for our fifteen- and sixteen-year-olds will take many years to establish for the same reason.

The major weakness in school-based curriculum development is the difficulty involved in turning theory into practice. So often new ideas and approaches are badly distorted by reliance on teachers who were trained, and resources that were developed, for completely different approaches. The introduction of mixed-ability is an outstanding example of this. Established originally on the traditional textbook and the teacher trained for a different approach, its acceptance has been limited, its implementation is often less effective than it might be, and its reputation has become controversial. Nuffield Science, on the other hand, developed many of its resources first and its acceptance throughout the education system was more assured as a result of that.

If curricular developments within the individual school need new and differently presented or structured materials, there is undoubtedly a danger that even a valuable initiative will prove less effective than it might and have too many difficulties to overcome to be sure of survival. This leads one almost inevitably to the conclusion that school-based development should either be restricted to initiatives that supplement or modify already existing regional or national developments, or, where there is a need and justification for much fuller treatment, that greater provision for central support at regional or national level should exist. Given the close link between in-service training and school-based curriculum development, teachers' centres, Local Authorities and Colleges and Departments of Education could provide for the latter alongside the former, with the most successful initiatives being developed nationally under the aegis of the Schools Council.

I return finally to extend earlier comparisons, albeit oversimplified, between the teaching and the medical profession. The doctor can add to and build on a range of techniques that have been modified and sophisticated. He does not have to start almost from the beginning again equipped with only the theory. To some extent the medical training institutions and those consultants involved are the custodians of the professional wisdom and experience that has accumulated over many years. The literature is a literature of theory turned into accepted practice and techniques.

Rightly or wrongly, the teacher starts at no such advanced point. At best it is the publisher who acts as custodian of the accumulated wisdom and experience of the profession turned into practice, and the majority of available resources have either served their day or are a personal, rather than professional, collection of resources and techniques. To be given any chance of being able to build on the present into the future, the new teacher, finding his way from theory to practice, needs to be able to choose from a far greater and more varied range of resources, continually being updated by central collaborative curriculum development groups at the regional or national level, so that he may almost always have something that can be modified to suit his purpose. The time and energies devoted to school-based curriculum development in so many separate schools could then be concentrated much more on meeting the needs of pupils and staff in a particular school by the redeployment, modification or supplementation of resources that already exist for the purpose, rather than being dissipated in the creation of those resources.

Acknowledgments

I am grateful to Tom Thompson, and particularly Rod Hill, for all their help with, and advice on, the resources included.

Chapter 5

The development of a Humanities curriculum at Manor Park School

Patrick Eavis

Manor Park School is an 11-18 comprehensive school of 1,000 pupils in the east of Newcastle. It is a split-site school: the Upper School (Years 3-6) in a 1960 building and the Lower School (Years 1-2) in a 1904 building a mile and a half away. The school was formed in 1967 by the merger of a selective technical school and three secondary modern schools. Over half the intake is from Social Priority primary schools.

Like many comprehensive schools it was founded on the assumption that the best curriculum organisation and content was to be found in the former grammar schools. From the start the grammar school was the model. This meant all the conventional subjects were taught separately from the first year, mostly in 35-minute periods. The children were banded in three ability bands but in the second year a class that took a second foreign language became almost a top set.

Following my appointment at Easter 1974 I felt that I should spend the first year observing, before introducing change, but I sensed that the staff expected change immediately. In my first weeks in the school I called meetings of each department separately, where I asked the Head of Department to start the discussion by outlining current policy. At each meeting I asked how staff saw the work of their department developing and what changes they would like to see. From these meetings I gained a reasonable impression of what was currently happening and some of the ways in which development was possible. It became obvious to me that tinkering with the existing system was no good, and that what was required was a radical change, which should be introduced in the first year and then work through the school. Extensive discussions at all levels, departmental, with Heads of Departments, and general staff meetings, confirmed that this was the right approach. We were already in the summer term and some changes would be introduced for the new entry in September.

Every school is different and the solutions of one may be inappropriate

116

to another. In my original discussion papers for staff I outlined general principles that seemed relevant to our situation. Thinking of our Lower School it seemed that the phreneticism in the lives of many of the children was mirrored in the school organization. The children were leaving the relative security of a small primary school where they had, for the most part, one teacher, and moving into a situation where they had over a dozen different teachers, where the bell was always ringing, and where they were constantly on the move. How could they relate to their teachers and each other? Was the constant movement making it impossible to establish the calm and quiet necessary for learning to take place? Further, were not the divisive consequences of streaming a contributory factor in disturbing the social health of the school? In any case, it seems impossible to justify early rigid streaming in a comprehensive school, one of whose *raisons d'être* was to prevent early selection. So I proposed:

1 Groupings of subjects for the Lower School: Combined Science, Humanities, Mathematics, Creative Arts, etc.
2 Mixed-ability organisation (including 'remedial' children)
3 Block time-tabling

The Humanities organisation

It was against this background that the Lower School Humanities organisation started. The English, Geography, History and Religious Education departments agreed to combine. The particular grouping owes less to epistemological reasons than to an accident of personalities. It is, for example, questionable whether the traditional alliance of History and Geography is ideal. Perhaps Geography is better placed in the sciences with Chemistry and Biology. And the linking of English with other subjects seems always fraught with difficulties. But these departments agreed to combine to produce a situation where first- and second-year pupils would have one teacher for all their subjects, which would amount to one teacher for a quarter of their time in school.

The preparatory discussions of staff involved in the new Humanities course showed that through a curricular change a new approach to teaching would have to be fashioned. There would be an end to the private world of the teacher. An end to the situation where the teacher disappears into a classroom to sink or swim, shielded by notions of the autonomy of the teacher, and a poster over the glass in the door. The new model presupposed group preparation, group evaluation, team teaching, collective responsibility.

This is one of the most essential priorities in staff organisation in comprehensive schools. The problems to overcome to teach effectively in mixed-ability classes in city comprehensive schools are such that it cannot be done single-handed. The horrific stories young teachers tell of their early experiences in comprehensive schools, for example, in *The First Year of Teaching*,[1] are partly the product of the old assumption that the teacher should be left alone to work out his own salvation: a misjudgment with which so many teachers collude, out of embarrassment, and understandable anxiety that they may more obviously be seen to fail. To overcome this an organisation which forces teachers to work together is essential. Not only is this necessary for survival, but, much more important, for growth, where every planning meeting is an element of in-service training. The mixture of expertise and experience in a large department is perhaps the richest resource for potential teacher development in a school, and often the least drawn upon.

The initial discussions among the Humanities staff concentrated on curriculum content. Should an attempt be made to integrate all the constituent subjects by working on themes which would involve a significant contribution from each of them? Such an approach is best seen, for example, in publications such as those of the Keele Integrated Studies Project. This was rejected in favour of a more traditional subject-based approach. It was felt that each subject's particular logic and skills could be lost in an integrated approach, so the staff opted for a programme of subject-based themes, of about six weeks each, chosen by the respective departments, with English Language work continuing all the time. This decision probably also reflected a traditional anxiety of secondary school subject specialists, who, unlike their less specialised trained primary school colleagues, feel worried about moving out of their subject field. Moreover, they feel uneasy about the prospect of the 'pure' content of their subject discipline being mixed with content of another discipline. And the decision of the Humanities staff points to an uneasy tension which has always been part of the working of the Humanities team. That is, how can subject needs and subject specialist staff be best accommodated in a combined subjects approach? The detailed organisation of the Humanities course is an attempt to provide a satisfactory solution.

Building modifications

When planning a major curriculum change all factors have to be taken into account, not least the buildings. So much hoped-for change comes unstuck at this point. Ideal schemes are worked out but their operation is so often hampered, if not effectively destroyed, by building layout. It is therefore vital to plan around the existing building allowing only for modifications which can definitely be introduced, which in days of financial stringency are almost nil.

Our building dates from 1904 and is designed to a pattern which can be seen in most old city schools. In the main block of the school there are two floors with a central hall on each, with rooms leading off. The lower hall is used for assemblies, youth clubs, etc., and so has only a limited use within the time-table. It was on the first floor of this building that we decided to locate the Humanities teaching. Previously, as with so many schools still, there were no recognised subject bases, which makes anything other than the most archaic teaching methods impossible.

The upper hall was not used as anything other than a vast corridor into which noisy children seemed to pour every 35 minutes. The library was a classroom with most miserable provision, totally inadequate for the 400 children in the building. Moreover, for most of the time it was locked and was only used for library periods. It was certainly never used as a place of reference during other lessons. The reallocation of the space in this area had to be in accordance with the needs of the Humanities teachers, but, on the other hand, their needs could not exceed the limitations of the buildings. The new design of the premises was perhaps the first major achievement of the Humanities team, but, of course, their decisions in this area were completely determined by the kind of curriculum and methods they had decided to implement.

Because it had been decided to introduce team teaching, and resource-based learning, facilities to allow this had to be created. The plans below show the original layout of the buildings, seven classrooms, a central hall, and various small rooms off on half-landings and the layout after conversion to the Humanities Centre.

The modification was simple. We removed the wall between rooms 2 and 3 to provide a space large enough to accommodate 100 pupils for team teaching. This essential space has 100 chairs already set out and it has all the audio-visual equipment necessary: slide projector, 16mm projector, screen, television set, cassette video-tape recorder, blackout. A lead lesson, therefore, takes no time to organise, 100 children can be in the room at a moment's notice and all the necessary equipment is at hand. The same applies if any single class wishes to use the equipment. It was well known to all of us that the under-use of audio-visual equipment by teachers does not arise in most cases from anything other than the sheer physical difficulties of getting it all organised. To have a place permanently set up, within easy reach of all classes, seems to us to be a top priority in the allocation of space in a school.

The inadequacy of the existing library accommodation for any plans to move to resource-based learning were obvious. It was therefore decided that the central hall should become the library resources centre. Since all classrooms lead off it it was ideally placed. Anxieties about security had to be allayed. To people brought up on locked libraries the transition to a library through which children would have to pass constantly,

119

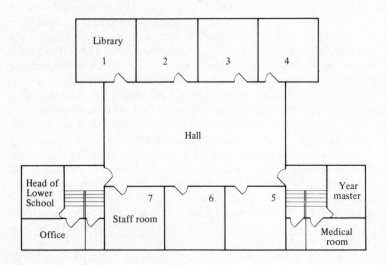

Figure 5.1a *Lower School first floor before conversion*

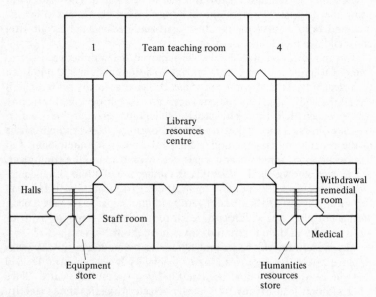

Figure 5.1b *Lower School first floor after conversion to Humanities Centre*

and which could not be locked, was almost too great to accept. But since the Newcastle Local Education Authority provides school librarians the problem of supervision is minimal. Moreover, to children, most of whom do not come from an environment in which books are important, the placing of the library centrally, through which they have to go constantly, is seen as positive reinforcement of the importance of books.

In the event, the moving of the library into the central hall proved to be the most significant physical change. The whole character of the building was transformed by it. From being a noisy open space and thoroughfare it has become a quiet, civilised, centre. It is carpeted, and that is vitally important. There is adequate light shelving, and banks of resource trays for housing the ever increasing quantities of teacher-produced non-book resources. Projector slides are stored in sheets in filing cabinets as are small equipment, cassette players, slide viewers, etc. The secret of the whole organisation of this area is that everything needed for teaching and learning is within a few yards of everyone, pupils and teachers, working in the area. Pupils wishing to use cassette recorders or viewers in the library can do so in the study carrels provided at the east end of the library.

One remaining room is used as the Lower School staffroom, while the other four are classrooms. On the east half-landing there is a secure store for stationery and night storage of valuable equipment. On the west half-landing is a small room for remedial withdrawal groups.

Time-table organisation

A further hazard in the way of successful curriculum innovation can be poor time-table organisation. But teams of teachers must realise that there are limitations to what can possibly be organised, factors which become more severe with the huge constraint of a split site. It is hopeless if teachers make plans for curriculum development if they are not aware of possible constraints. This calls for consultation all along with the time-tablers, which is not to say that the time-tablers call the tune, but that all involved understand the mutual problems and that excellent ideal schemes are not worked out and later found to be impracticable. We are now working on a scheme where the time-tabler produces a model which the teachers themselves staff, so that any compromises that have to be made are seen to be necessary by the teachers concerned, and the department itself decides its own priorities in coming to those compromises.

Below is a copy of the current Lower School time-table. There are six classes in each year group which are divided into two teams of three classes which are always time-tabled together. Every period is one hour,

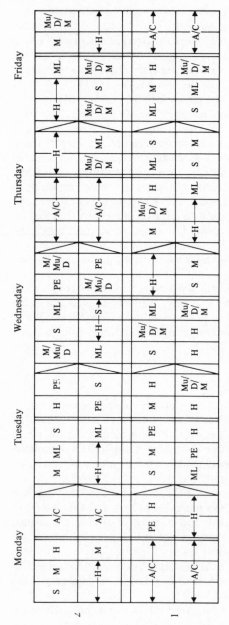

Figure 5.2

There were originally four classes of 25 in each half-year group. Now, owing to falling numbers, there are three.

and in Arts and Crafts and Humanities periods are often longer than this. Our time-table is far from ideal because we have to deal with the constraints of a split site where all the staff move between the sites. However, most of our main priorities are achieved; time-tabling in half-year groups making team teaching possible, giving larger blocks of time to subjects that want them, cutting down the number of teachers any one group would see in a week, and minimising movement of pupils.

Staffing

It was originally decided to divide both First and Second Years into two groups with approximately 100 pupils in each. The half-year group was then divided into four classes. We thought it important to keep the class size as low as possible to give mixed-ability grouping the best chance of being successful. This was achieved partly by the generous Newcastle staffing ratios, partly by the commitment of 'administrative' staff to more teaching than is usually the case (I teach nearly a half time-table), but also by the decision to use two extra staff that the Local Education Authority gave every school for a disruptive unit to help keep classes smaller in order to help prevent disruptive behaviour at source. So we have no disruptive unit, and in the Lower School an almost negligible incidence of disruptive behaviour. The phenomenal improvement in behaviour is partly the result of smaller classes but also the result of team teaching and co-operation, where teachers talk about their problems and help each other with potential trouble-makers by such strategies as taking another's difficult pupil for a time. But in this critical area the positive results of genuinely working together are so clear. (See HMI good-practice discussion document on disruptive behaviour and truancy.[2])

The composition of the two teams in each year-group mirrors as far as possible the constituent subject disciplines in Humanities: that is an English specialist, Historian, Geographer, and Religious Education specialist. This would mean that in the course of any subject theme there would always be a specialist on the spot. Over the past four years it has not always been possible to keep exactly this distribution, and, now, owing to declining numbers, we have had to reduce the teams to three classes in each.

The organisation of subject content

Since the work in Humanities is usually approached thematically the subject specialists in the teams are responsible for choosing the themes and preparing the work programme for the whole of the theme. They say what the aims and objectives of the theme are and suggest a variety of work and teacher approaches that will lead to their achievement.

Here is an example of the aims and objectives statement for a theme prepared by the Geography Department. Like all introductory statements of themes distributed to other members of the teams it includes reasons for including the theme, key geographical concepts, and skills to be developed by the work on the theme.

The earth in space

This particular theme was chosen to start the year because
  (a) it provides a logical starting point for the study of geography in the secondary school
  (b) it is a topic that facilitates the development of basic geographical skills and study skills
  (c) it is interesting in itself

Key concepts

1 The earth is only a small planet in a vast universe
2 Distances in the universe are so large that it is convenient to measure them in light years
3 The 'Big Bang' theory offers one explanation of the origin of the universe.
4 The sun's family of planets is called the Solar System
5 The earth is a planet of the sun
6 The earth cooled down from a ball of hot gas
7 The interior of the earth can be analysed and comprises crust, core, and mantle
8 The earth is spherical
9 Movement of the earth around the sun is responsible for day and night and the seasons
10 A world map is a projection, not a true copy of reality
11 Britain is located in Europe, which is just one of several continents
12 Geography is concerned with man in his environment and where things are in that environment

Skills:

Reference skills: (i) alphabetical order
                     (ii) use of encyclopaedia
                     (iii) atlas work
                     (iv) use of contents page
                     (v) types of book

	(vi) use of reference books
	(vii) geography of library
Measurement	(i) location – grid references
	(ii) of direction – points of compass
	(iii) of distance – linear measurement
	(iv) of scale – linear scale and RF

Within each theme the individual and class work is interrupted by lead lessons which happen roughly once a week. These give the subject specialist an opportunity to organise a lesson for the whole half-year group. The lead lessons vary immensely and are always extremely well prepared and professional in their presentation. A theatre theme in English included visits spaced weekly of a drama group, ballet dancers, a mime artist. A History theme on Slavery lasting for five weeks included the following lead lessons:

Slavery – lead lesson programme

1 Origins of the Slave Trade – slides, tape and explanation
2 Dramatised slave auction using staff and pupils followed by discussion
3 Beliefs of slaves from negro spirituals. Staff and pupils playing and singing
4 Plantation life. Slides and explanation
5 Wilberforce and the Campaign for Abolition. Slides/overhead projector and explanation

All workbooks, workcards, assignments, etc., are prepared for at least three different ability-levels, and the Remedial Department produces resources on each theme for the very slow readers. The department organising the theme makes suggestions of the way in which the different prepared materials can be used. This information is circulated and discussed. The recommendations in Figure 5.3 were for a theme about the Jews. Triangles indicate work for the most able, rectangles work for average pupils, and circles, work for the less able.

The other members of the team often contribute in supplying extra related work where there are overlaps between subjects, for example, on the History theme 'Ancient Greeks' the geographers produced work on the location of Greek cities, and the Religious Education specialist did the same for Greek religion. The English specialists always suggest ways in which the subject material can be used to develop English skills but they also supply English Language assignments to tie in with each theme. Because we were concerned that language across the curriculum should become a reality, we organised our own in-school, in-service training programme for Humanities teachers. Frequently we hear doubts

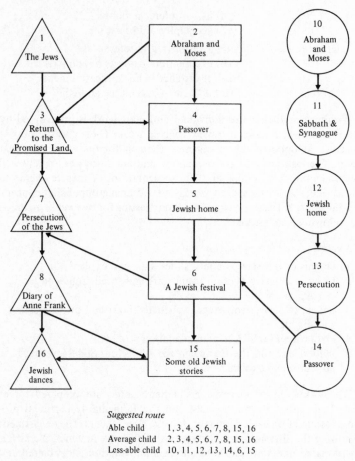

Figure 5.3

expressed from outside that English Language skills suffer in a Humanities-type organisation. Our experience is that it provides a unique opportunity to implement the Bullock recommendations across a quarter of the curriculum, and the evidence of our own testing indicates that language skills improve considerably in the first two years (see Bristol Achievement Test results discussed later).

The preparation of resources and organisation for a theme is an enormous undertaking, and preparation at that level could not be achieved by a teacher working on his own. But because of the team preparation it means that, say, the Geographers only have to produce two themes in each year. For the rest of the time they will be operating with materials mostly prepared by their colleagues. So the standard of the teacher-produced material is high because teachers have time enough to produce it, but also because they realise that their work has to be used by others.

This kind of organisation presupposes a high degree of prior discussion and consultation among team members. These are regular meetings where the preparation of the next theme is discussed and guidance and discussion are undertaken on the current theme. These meetings are more like training seminars than briefing meetings. From time to time outside 'experts' are invited to lead discussions. An ex-College of Education senior lecturer on the staff has done work on English teaching, and Head of Newcastle Remedial Service has helped, as have relevant Local Education Authority subject advisers. Since we avoid distinctions of academic and pastoral responsibilities Humanities teachers have had in-school, in-service guidance on caring for individual needs which was led by two lecturers from the Polytechnic Counselling course. The Humanities team is not only concerned about subject content and organisation of lessons but accepts the total responsibility for the children while they are in the area. One of the first things the team did four years ago was to draw up an agreed list of basic rules that they should all enforce. It took a Saturday morning to decide what they should be, and it has been a troublesome area ever since, and always will be. The cartoon (Figure 5.4) was produced by one of the Humanities team as a comment on a fairly recent meeting considering the same points. Since the current theme was Ancient Greece the comment was made in appropriate terms.

Plus ça change, plus c'est la même chose

All the figures in the cartoon are recognisable as members of the Humanities team and it refers to the difference of opinion about, among other things, how strict the rules for the whole Humanities area should be.

Resources for learning

Since the grouping in Lower School Humanities is mixed-ability it was decided that the teaching and learning strategies should be individualised as much as possible. This implied the collection and production of vast resources. Clearly this could only be possible with co-operative planning, and without secretarial help it would certainly founder. The will to work together was there and the secretarial help was made available by employing two part-time secretaries instead of one laboratory assistant. They now run a reprographics centre and are exclusively used in work for the staff: typing, duplicating, doing graphic work, radio and CCTV recording. It always amazes me how many schools run on the assumption

Figure 5.4

that individualised work schemes are ideal and yet make no provision to prepare them. And even with the kind of co-operative planning and sharing of resources we have in all departments, without secretarial help the burden on staff would be impossible. If it came to the point we would sooner lose a part of a teacher than this secretarial help.

The dangers of worksheet methods are now widely publicised. We have always been aware of this even though sometimes our practice would not indicate that.

The inadequacy of traditional methods having been realised by many teachers they sought salvation through the typewriter. The theory went something like this: talking does not work because it is impossible to make them listen, so replace the spoken word with a barrage of work-sheets to keep the troops too busy to riot. They abound in many schools, sheet after sheet of dreary typewritten and duplicated pages. Brunel on one side, Stephenson on the other, now on to Free Trade. And the reward for finishing one worksheet is the offer of another.

Perhaps such methods at first help with problems of control. But the children soon tire of worksheets and the temptation to turn them into paper darts becomes less resistible. What is needed is a balance between individual work and classwork, and as much variety as it is possible to introduce. A theme on the Middle Ages, for example, involves lead lessons, workbooks, project cards, a tape-slide sequence, a video cassette recorder film, library assignments, suggestions for discussions, work on documents. Art work also provides variety. The following is advice to colleagues for art work on a slavery theme.

Ideas for art work in Humanities

Note: It would be a good idea if you told the others what you are doing so that there is not too much repetition.

Theme: *Slavery and the American Civil War*

1 *Guineamen collage*: Large-scale slave ship to pin on blue boards in library. Hull — corrugated cardboard, masts — strips of paper, ropes - string and sails — pieces of white material cut to shape
2 *Triangular trade map*: Large scale — cutting out land masses and pinning on blue notice board. Figures and ships — cardboard cut-outs backed with empty match boxes to give relief effect
3 *Slave coffle*: Black cut-out profiles i.e. silhouettes of slaves (each child does a slave — scale kept regular by cutting paper to size and making child fill the whole paper). Chains linking silhouettes — circles of string, perhaps set on red or yellow paper
4 *Slave ship*: Using coiled clay make hull of ship. Stick match sticks into hull as slatted shelves and make slaves in clay to lie on them. (Use diagrams from worksheets to work from)
5 *Posters*: Design old style slave posters — pro-slavery and modern style anti-slavery posters. Old style emphasising lettering, modern emphasising drawing/painting — minimum of words — could use slogan mentioned in Wilberforce worksheet
6 *Topsy*: Life-size painting or collage (use child to draw round)

7 *Confed. uniform*: Life-size painting or collage (after lead lesson on uniforms perhaps?)

8 *Frieze of battle*: Using same method as No. 3 for scale regularity. Each child does three soldiers in crayon or paint — 1 standing, 1 kneeling, 1 lying down — one class could do confederates the other unions. (For epic effect one half-year group against another)

Library assistance

Since the library resources area is central to our work the organisation of the library is critical. The Newcastle Local Education Authority provides a trained librarian shared between two comprehensive schools, with sufficient assistants to ensure that there is a librarian permanently in each library. The library staff are seen as part of the teaching team. They attend all planning meetings and ensure that the relevant resources are conveniently organised for the current theme. They also catalogue all non-book resource materials, and ensure that workbooks, cards, worksheets, etc., are properly stored in tray units for the easy access of staff and pupils. Because they have been involved in all aspects of planning, the librarians are able to give a much better service to the children in each theme. More than this, at the start of each first year the library staff take a major role in the initial library training course. Their continued involvement throughout the year ensures the constant reinforcement of the skills they have taught. We put it as a very high priority among the skills that First and Second Year children should have acquired that they should be able to use the Library. My own experience of teaching Third Year pupils when they move to the Upper School is that this has happened, and how much easier life for all of us is as a result.

Remedial provision

From the beginning, Humanities staff have agreed that it is preferable to have a full range of ability in each class including so-called remedial children. There is no separate remedial class as there is in many schools. Children are withdrawn for remedial help individually or in small groups, but the problem is: when? Originally such children were withdrawn during Humanities lessons, but the staff felt this was a mistake. But if they are to have extra help, when should they get it, for the arguments about missing Humanities lessons apply equally to all other subjects? Two possible solutions have been tried. One, to have remedial experts coming into Humanities lessons. This, however, has proved less successful than giving children help away from the classroom. So we now take all the Modern Languages time for remedial children. It is an unhappy, but perhaps realistic, compromise.

During Humanities lessons remedial children work on the same themes as all other children with materials devised partly by remedial staff who are a part of the Humanities team. Since there is free movement around the whole area it is possible for children to go to the remedial room during Humanities lessons if they need special help, and this happens frequently. But it must never be forgotten that there are many activities in which remedial children can easily share: lead lessons, drama, discussion, model making, listening to tape-slide sequences, etc. And if the written work is individually planned and directed there is no reason to separate such children.

Assessment

When we set up the Humanities course and mixed-ability organisation there was pressure from the governing body to assess our performance. This was seen to be especially important in progress in English since the Humanities organisation meant a different approach to English teaching. We thought we should apply some external objective test as a measure of our progress and opted for the Bristol Achievement Test. The choice was made of this test primarily because it was recommended by a Senior Lecturer from the almost adjacent College of Education who was working very closely with us with his students at that time. He was prepared to administer the test the first time as an exercise for his students. This, too, became an in-school, in-service training project for the staff.

The tests are achievement tests in English, Mathematics and Study Skills. Our results over the past three years show a consistent improvement in all subjects. We would have been content if pupils held their own from First to Second Year since an average score at Level 5 similar to that of Level 4 suggests progress at a normal rate because the individual scores on which the average is based are age-corrected. In fact, there is a significant percentage improvement in achievement overall and it is interesting to note that there has been slightly more improvement in English, taught as part of Humanities course in mixed-ability classes, than there has been in Mathematics taught in sets.

Table 5.1 shows the score comparison of whole classes in the Second Year (1978) with their results in the First Year (1977). In each class considerably more pupils have made gains in their performance than have lost ground, and this point is much more clearly made if one reads the second column in each set of figures, where we use the more statistically significant number of a 5-point rise or fall in achievement.

Table 5.2 (p. 133) shows the comparative results 1976–7 of one class.

TABLE 5.1

	English				Maths				Study skills			
Forms	Higher scores		Lower scores		Higher scores		Lower scores		Higher scores		Lower scores	
	+1	*+5*	*−1*	*−5*	*+1*	*+5*	*−1*	*−5*	*+1*	*+5*	*−1*	*−5*
C	15	12	3	1	14	10	6	3	14	13	5	4
H	17	12	7	1	11	7	10	4	15	2	5	–
I	14	10	4	1	15	10	5	3	13	9	6	2
L	15	10	7	2	17	9	5	3	15	6	6	3
D	15	8	7	4	14	9	7	4	14	8	8	3
R	20	14	5	1	16	13	4	2	17	11	8	5
E	13	8	9	5	10	4	6	3	10	6	7	3
N	15	7	4	3	12	7	9	3	16	10	6	1

Note: The figures in the +5/−5 columns are naturally incorporated in the +1/−1 columns

Notes

1 C. Hannam *et al.*, *The First Year of Teaching*, Harmondsworth, Penguin, 1976.
2 'Truancy and behavioural problems in some urban schools', Department of Education and Science, 1978.

Table 5.2 (p. 133) shows the comparative results 1976-7 of one class.

	English 1976		English 1977		Maths 1976		Maths 1977		Study skills 1976		Study skills 1977	
	Standard-ised score	Per-centile	Standard-ised score	Per-centile	Standard-ised score	Per-centile	Standard-ised score	Per-centile	Standard-ised score	Per-centile	Standard-ised score	Per-centile
Susan	94	34	90	25	81	10	82	11	74	4	83	13
Wendy	94	34	104	61	81	10	99	48	95	37	91	27
Diane	72	3	82	11	74	4	82	11	91	27	83	13
Julie	109	73	106	66	103	58	114	82	100	50	105	63
Tracey	99	48	100	50	92	30	98	45	99	48	98	45
Lesley	93	32	99	48	94	34	93	32	79	8	91	27
Julie	72	3	76	5	76	5	78	7	77	6	78	7
Paula	120	91	122	93	112	79	107	68	109	73	114	82
Anne	100	50	106	66	95	37	96	39	86	18	90	25
Karen	113	81	115	84	94	34	99	48	100	50	102	55
John	103	58	101	52	103	58	106	66	106	66	109	73
Carl	73	4	60		69	2	75	5	60		76	5
Christopher	98	45	104	61	96	39	108	70	96	39		
Shaun	86	18	86	18	78	7	83	13	60		85	16
Jonathan	91	27	93	32	92	30	82	11	90	25	92	30
Thomas	92	30	90	25	83	13	89	24	85	16	104	61
Brian	86	18	100	50	95	37	105	63	97	42	111	76
Stephen	109	73	106	66	96	39	104	61	99	48	104	61
Juswant	118	88	115	84	101	52	113	81	115	84	110	75
Gary	96	39	99	48	107	68	107	68	109	73	107	68
Robert	60	1	84	14	69	2	83	13	60		88	21
George	72	3	78	7	72	3	60		82	11	95	37
Kevin	92	30	96	39	89	24	103	58	96	39	105	63

Chapter 6

Language through the curriculum at Hele's School

Peter Cloke

In this chapter, I outline two major school-based curriculum projects. Both arose in recognition of specific needs of pupils within the school; the first had the added incentive of a national report.

In 1972, Hele's School, in Devon, began to change its status from an old-established grammar school to a comprehensive school for boys aged 12–16. One of the major problems was the language difficulties being encountered by many new pupils. The language of the mass of the textbooks existing in the school was often far too difficult; how did one attempt to match a worksheet to a boy's reading age? What criteria were to be used in assessing written work? How much talking – and of what kind – did we allow in our lessons? There was much informal conversation in the staff room about these 'new' problems.

In 1975, the Bullock Report[1] came as a catalyst to our thinking, offering a clear sense of direction: 'every school should have an organised policy for language across the curriculum, establishing every teacher's involvement in language and reading development throughout the years of schooling.' So much of our curriculum depends on the pupil's ability to handle language in its various forms in the secondary school that Bullock's insistence on the need for a school language policy seemed realistic. Hele's did have a language policy, although it was far from manifest. How could an implicit concern for language be made more explicit? Beginning with existing 'non-policy' seemed to offer the most promising start, asking teachers to talk about what went on behind the closed classroom door. How could these doors be opened and subject boundaries crossed, tensions resolved and natural suspicions overcome?

These barriers and suspicions had, to some extent, been broken down by a strongly led school-based Area Training Organisation/Department of Education and Science course in 1974–5; colleagues had visited each other's classrooms and shared their reactions with twenty or so other course members. Keen interest and support had come from Local

Education Authority advisory staff; positive encouragement and involvement came from the Head and his deputies. This openness to suggestion and criticism based on exchange of method and views were to prove key factors in planning the work towards developing a language policy in the school.

The first stage of the project was to identify recurrent themes in the informal conversations which had taken place up to this time and to consider ways in which action could be taken. Ideas were summarised and produced in a paper which was introduced at a meeting of the school's senior staff. Particular attention was given to what Bullock had called 'the relative neglect of talk as a means of learning'. Was a noisy classroom seen as a threat to the teacher's authority? Could we identify 'a language of the subject'? What special demands did our own subjects make in written and spoken language, and what were we doing about them? Was it realistic to leave responsibility for development of language skills to the English Department? In fact, the time a pupil spends using language outside the classroom vastly outweighs the two and half hours or so he is under the guidance of an English teacher each week. This suggested a fundamental shift in responsibility for language development; spelling, note-taking, summary and presentation are seen as writing skills to be developed in all subject areas, as are skills in clear exposition, in talk as well as writing.

The paper received a sympathetic response and was duplicated and distributed to all staff. A series of meetings was suggested, to consider some of the issues raised. Should these meetings carry the status of a full staff meeting with all the staff expected to attend, or purely voluntary for those colleagues who saw language problems as an area of prime concern in the curriculum? If only a small group of staff turned up at the meetings, how could one ensure the vital awareness of the whole staff? It was felt that the heavy hand of authoritative suggestion, needed to promote an almost full attendance at a meeting of the whole staff, was not only inappropriate in the light of the leadership style within the school but also would have failed to take into account the different priorities which teachers have in schools. Alienation could easily have occurred – the last thing one would want in an attempt to establish language through the curriculum. The project, in its probing of current practice within the school, would need to be tentative in its approach to some sensitive issues. There had to be a balance between catering for individual teachers' needs and making the work of sufficient interest and relevance to capture the imagination of the whole staff. The project had to be credible professionally if ideas were to be taken seriously by them.

All colleagues were individually invited to attend meetings due to start in June. At this stage of term, colleagues would have a little more time to spare. Minutes of meetings would be circulated to all staff.

135

Some ten fortnightly meetings took place during the summer and autumn terms 1976. In their planning and structure they were similar: colleagues from different subject areas would work together in a language 'workshop' which, after a short introduction, would involve a shared practical activity followed by a plenary session.

Perhaps the most pressing problems were centred on reading difficulties; three sessions were devoted to work on readability and ways of developing different reading strategies. Colleagues were introduced to readability scales and spent some time assessing reading ages demanded by a range of textbooks and worksheets in use in the school. Much of the material was found to presume a high reading age; some guidance was given by a member of the remedial department on how to simplify texts.

There was a change of emphasis after these three meetings. About half the staff had attended the early meetings and many of them felt that it would be valuable to highlight the language problems posed in the classroom by experiencing these difficulties first-hand. Two Heads of Department offered to lead sessions where the rest of the group would be treated as 'learners' — to be exposed to the language demands in two areas of the school's curriculum. Detailed reports of the two meetings were circulated to all colleagues as follows:

Meeting (5): September 29th, 1976 in the Science Lab.

'The Significance of Language in the Science Lesson'

BWS opened the meeting by stating that his objective for this session was to highlight some of the ways language was used in the work of the Science Department. He wanted the group to judge the effectiveness of language used on the worksheets and to show the group how he encouraged talk, based on experiments.

The worksheets were to be used with 3rd year mixed ability groups. They had been subjected to analysis of readability by the *Cloze procedure* (see minutes of meeting 2, 30.6.76) and JFS had found that the two worksheets had reading ages of ten and eleven respectively.

The two worksheets were based on the concepts of *Energy* and *Forces*.

BWS then demonstrated various experiments designed to show that energy could not be created or destroyed and that it could easily be changed from one form to another. He moved on to show the group pieces of equipment used in the Force experiments.

He then invited the group to examine whether or not this type of work was valuable in helping pupils with their development of language. Was the work sufficiently demanding to tax the 'high flier' and yet sufficiently easy for the less-able? Were the ensuing work-sheets of any use to the non-reader?

The rest of the session was spent in discussing some of the many issues raised. Amongst the topics considered were:

The Use of Questions — BWS emphasised the value of well directed questions during experiments — and the importance of considering points orally before writing about them.

Should questions be graded? It was felt that this might be a way to cope with the wide range of ability in the group.

Was the Worksheet approach more valuable than 'Chalk and Talk'? BWS felt that he was able to give more attention to the less-able when pupils were working from worksheets.

Vocabulary — how did the less-able cope with scientific jargon? How much emphasis was given to consideration of the teacher's own language?

Assessment — how could this type of work be monitored? Was any test of recall of facts made? BWS said that this was done through teachers' marking at present, but that he was considering additional safeguards.

Groupings — was any attempt made to group according to different abilities? BWS said that he was satisfied with the 'friendship' groups which worked well together.

Inference and Evaluation —DHW suggested that additional questions could be set to encourage a more open-ended, essay type response. BWS said that he was particularly keen to encourage this type of creative work in science.

At the end of the session BWS said that he had valued the pooling of ideas and suggestions and the group thanked him for providing such a positive and interesting session.

Meeting (6): October 13th, 1976 in the Language Lab.

'The Problems of Comprehension in Modern Language Teaching'

MJO's aim in this session was to treat the group as a class of beginners learning Italian. He hoped that the group would experience some of the comprehension and language difficulties normally encountered by the pupils.

The first part of the 'Lezione d'Italiano' was spent in learning numbers in Italian, followed by a study of the Italian names of members of the family, using flash card stimulus. The group carried out a variety of demanding oral and written tasks. After discussion of some of the issues raised, MJO introduced a transcript of a radio programme which had proved popular with his classes, and the group was invited to follow the transcript as a tape-recording of the pro-gramme was relayed.

During the discussion many interesting points were raised:

1 *How important is the impact of the written word?* DGM and MRL reflected on their own experience by stating that they felt it was vital to *see* as well as *hear* the words being learned. MJO suggested that it was vital for fluency and understanding to *hear* before *seeing*; this was especially important for less-able pupils.

2 *How did the teacher deal with individual difficulties?* DHW expressed concern for the pupil who had fallen behind in some aspects of the work. MJO agreed that a regular and systematic assessment of an individual's progress was vital; hopefully any difficulties could be re-worked with an individual as the rest of the class worked at written assignments. He stressed the importance of pupils realising that they were making progress and the need for teachers to structure positive mark schemes to give each pupil some degree of success.

3 *Should children of all abilities study French?* It was suggested that pupils with a V.R.Q. of 70 or more could study a foreign language with a degree of success. JFS pointed out that this test should not be regarded as an absolute assessment of an individual's ability, and that several of his pupils from remedial groups were enjoying French and gaining much from work with an oral emphasis.

4 *What sort of talk situations could occur in the modern languages lesson?* DHW pointed out that in our lesson we had experienced many of the skills in concentration and talk that would be useful in all subject areas. MJO emphasised the importance of 'structured' talk – and the necessity for tight organisation of oral sessions.

5 *How does grouping of pupils influence the quality of talk?* After some discussion of the problems of getting pupils in the 4th and 5th year to respond orally, BWS suggested that in oral work the more able pupils in the 4th and 5th years did not respond as well as the less able, and a possible alternative to setting would be to teach in mixed-ability groups. MJO said that he was in sympathy with this approach but was faced with the practical problems of a shortened exam course – (four years instead of five) and the need for financial and staffing resources to implement such a course.

6 *What particular difficulties did the members of the group encounter?* There was some discussion of the problems of concentration when listening and how this could be affected by the teacher's speed and style of delivery.

The group also experienced some of the problems and pressures of being in a learning situation in a classroom. One's performance was so easily affected by the time of the day, effects of group hierarchy etc. How often do we allow for pupils' individual differences and difficulties in our own teaching?

More technical issues were introduced towards the end of the course. There was detailed consideration of the impact of print on the reader, followed by colleagues working together in planning layout of worksheets and booklet covers under the guidance of a member of the Art Department. An all too short session was spent attempting to formulate a common policy on setting out of written work. A member of the Remedial Department demonstrated equipment and methods used in developing language skills in the less able; the Head of the English Department in one of the school's largest feeder middle schools talked to the group about her school's approach to language development, stressing the important role of resources at the centre of her work.

At the end of the series of meetings it was evident that some areas had not been covered in sufficient depth. The special language problems of the less able had been discussed from the point of view of the Remedial Department but little consideration had been given to how different departments were attempting to adjust teaching styles and materials to those pupils who were receiving compensatory work in English and Maths but who were being taught in normal class groups for other subjects. 'Talk' had been an enigmatic topic, often referred to as being an essential prerequisite to successful learning, but perhaps inadequately tackled from the point of view of implementation of ideas in the classroom.

In an attempt to redress this balance and also to provide some background theory to the work which had gone on, a number of colleagues — Heads of Department and others — were asked to write papers which outlined their own department's approach to language development. Colleagues with special interest and relevant experience in the areas of talking and listening in the classroom and the relationship between language and drama were asked to write papers for inclusion in the booklet. A paper from our middle school colleague reminded us that the pupil's language background in his family and early schools was of critical importance. The booklet was concluded by a paper which suggested certain guidelines for resource development in language and learning. Copies of the booklet were sent to other secondary schools in the area, feeder middle schools and sixth-form college, as well as distributed to the whole staff.[2]

Contents

Headmaster's Overview	1
Talking and Listening in the Classroom	2
Language Development in the Science Lesson	3

The Special Language Problems of the Less Able 4
Language and Drama 5
The Humanities — Its Part in Language Development 6
Language Experience in Design for Living 7
Language and Thought 8
Development of the English Language Skills through the
    Teaching of a Foreign Language 9
Language in a Middle School 10
Resources for Language and Learning 11
Appendix   Introductory sheet
         Minutes of 10 meetings

The first theoretical paper 'Talking and Listening in the Classroom' envisaged a fundamental shift in role emphasis for the teacher: 'We must be free to circulate from group to group listening and participating, not with any authority derived from status, but with authority derived from being a mature and fluent user of language in the room.' The paper also raised some fundamental questions about talk in the classroom, the writer stressing the need for an environment which held a more equal balance between talking and writing as well as greater opportunities for pupils to listen to each other talking, not only to the teacher.

The writer of the paper on 'Language and Thought' began by outlining the progressive development of language skills. He moved on to consider the language of the teacher in his classroom and the possibilities of behavioural problems arising from the clash between teachers as users of an 'elaborated code' of language and pupils whose language use and understanding is in a 'restricted code'.

The short paper on 'Language and Drama' described the potential for a wide variety of language use in the drama lesson and discussed an experiment which offered a strong example of the way in which drama could enrich pupils' written language.

In his paper on resource development for language and learning, the writer aimed at two broad areas of written and audio-visual material, stressing the need to examine written material for the reading age demanded, plus types of comprehension asked for in the reader; audio-visual material needed to be relevant and suitable for a wide variety of language responses.

It was evident from subject Heads' contributions that there was a deepening awareness of the importance of language in their work; they also had a developing expertise in preparation and assessment of materials from the point of view of language response demanded. Colleagues had shared problems and listened to valued advice in moving towards a greater responsibility for language development in their own subject areas.

The next major impetus for a school-based course came from the Headmaster, in his recognition of the need to examine the school's provision for those pupils not receiving compensatory education but who were underachieving. These pupils were often vaguely classified by teachers as being 'below average' — not conspicuously handicapped but often failing to do as well as had been hoped.

The investigation has fallen into three stages; firstly, a member of the school's Remedial Department was asked to 'investigate learning problems affecting boys of low ability in normal departments' classes/ lessons in which the school's extraction system did not apply; to indicate common problems, and good practice where he saw it, in Hele's and elsewhere; to offer by June 1978 recommendations for action'. The second stage consisted of the writing of the report and its distribution amongst the staff; the third stage was discussion leading to decisions on the implementation of recommendations.

The crucial factor in staff acceptance of the scheme was that there was a general recognition of the need for action and a willingness to respond to it. Once again colleagues were to open their classrooms to scrutiny. There had been a positive lead within the school and encouragement and interest from Local Education Authority advisers.

The first task was to identify and subsequently list those pupils considered to be within the scope of the assignment. All subject teachers were asked to list such pupils under one or more arbitrary categories:

(i) backward — less able pupils of below average ability

(ii) retarded — under-achievers who were quite possibly of average intelligence

(iii) educationally maladjusted — in terms of poor behaviour and emotional instability

(iv) others — particularly discontinuous education cases

It was emphasised that these categories were merely tools to assist teachers to identify pupils, and to be used in later stages of the assignment. On receipt of the lists of pupils, profiles of individual pupils would be built up containing information from subject teachers, pastoral staff, test-score data and comments on attainment and potential. Individual profiles were then examined to identify common factors wherever possible; 'good practice' was identified and recorded — not only when it had been seen within the school, but also in other schools visited.

The writer of the report acknowledged the methodological criticisms which could be made of the course of action: 'It relied heavily on the subjective opinion of teachers, their interpretation of categories and on their personal ideologies and feelings.' He continued, in an attempt to justify his approach: 'It did offer a practical means of attempting to reach the objectives already outlined and it was realistic, given the enormity of the task and constraints of time.'

The investigation was introduced to a meeting of the senior staff in September 1977; individual Heads of Department were seen during the next two months. Some departments held special meetings to discuss arrangements for the implementation of the investigation; other Heads of Department decided to brief their own staff. Lists of pupils were returned and information collated.

It soon became apparent that more pupils were being listed than had been anticipated so it was decided to focus on a random sample of pupils from different year and subject groups for the purpose of detailed subject teachers' reports.

While this information was being collected, the investigation proceeded with informal interviews with subject teachers and Heads of Department. Another important part of the investigation was the accumulation of 'raw material' gathered from over fifty periods of lesson observation. The sample of lessons included some taught by Heads of Department as well as probationers and was seen as a critical part of the assignment, offering 'essential support and evidence' in the recommendations for action. Copies of textbooks and written material used regularly were obtained and various readability tests carried out on them.

The overall results came from two sources: the pupil profiles suggested certain identifiable factors within the school and gave some idea of the extent of the problem. Personal observation and discussion also suggested certain relevant factors from within subject areas.

The first significant factor to emerge from the profiles was the poor reading ability of some 79 per cent of the pupils listed, although intelligence scores, used with some reservations, suggested that many of them had average or above average intelligence. This perhaps suggested that pupils with learning difficulties were not predominantly those of low intelligence, as was often assumed. Other common factors began to emerge as a result of lesson observation. It was evident that many boys were being faced with material they could not be expected to read, especially in mixed-ability groups in Science and Humanities in the lower school. Examples were given which indicated that some material used presumed a reading age of three years or more in excess of chronological age. The neglect of talk as a means of learning in some classrooms was also noted, as was occasional use of overspecialised and inappropriate language on the part of the teacher. The reliance on 'the language of the subject' was commented upon: 'Excessive use of the language of a specialist subject, in text books as well as in speech tends to exclude all pupils exept those able to contemplate joining the specialist group.' The use of everyday words did not represent a lowering of standards but 'a matter of working to a less traditional standard'.

The transition from a primary school, modelled on independent learning, to a secondary school with a teacher-dominated, subject-centred approach was commented upon, the change being a 'sudden and traumatic' one for the able boy who could cope; for the boy with learning difficulties it was 'often disastrous'.

Detailed reports of individual departments and their own approaches to boys with learning difficulties then followed; teaching method and grouping strategy were discussed. Good practice was identified and commented upon – for example, staff in the Science and Humanities Departments were complimented on their creation of opportunities for talk to assist learning but the written report criticised them for sometimes failing to take advantage of such situations.

Specific recommendations for action were aimed at general educational provision within the school as well as individual departments. More substantial screening of each intake year was proposed and transfer of the information gained should be built into communication processes within the school. A 'reading unit' was suggested, where intensive tuition in basic reading skills could be given. A working party could usefully examine the range of option choices available to boys with learning difficulties.

The Remedial Department was seen as providing a central role in leading other departments in assessing readability as well as offering practical suggestions on resource development for materials to be used with boys with learning difficulties. It was suggested that all departments should scrutinise teaching approaches and language as well as the opportunities for purposeful talk in lesson time.

Reference was made to the earlier work on language and to the 'excellent suggestions' which many Heads of Department had made in the booklet; it was noted, though, that many of these suggestions were still in print and not in practice and a further course was proposed, concerned more specifically with the implementation of ideas. The English Department was seen as having a leading role here, giving colleagues guidance on the use of oral language for learning.

The report, then, suggested many possible areas for further school-based work; the inquiry into communication processes within the school, option courses and the use of oral language for learning are but three of them. It also implied allocation of finance and staff in the instigation of a 'reading unit'.

In its comment on the gap between stated intention and actual practice in the use of language for learning, the report also brought out problems of the institutionalisation of innovation. Hele's could certainly be called a 'creative' school in terms of its capacity for adaptation and generation of innovation, but perhaps more attention does need to be paid to what Hoyle has called the 'after care' of this innovation.[3] He provides a wider context in suggesting that 'although many British schools have been willing to introduce innovations, there have been

143

problems in their institutionalisation'. He links these problems, amongst other things, to lack of internal support within the school. One form this support could take is in the evaluation of what had been achieved in the classroom as a result of the innovation. Indeed Nisbet sees evaluation as a crucial part of 'any innovatory enterprise'.[4] The investigation into boys with learning difficulties and its ensuing report went some way to evaluating earlier work in the school. Its clear message was that future work at Hele's must focus on implementation. Stenhouse[5] has suggested that 'a new curriculum will never be secure until it accumulates round a tradition'. Creating this tradition and the right climate for change as well as developing adequate 'support systems' are all functions of leadership within the school.

Successful school-based curriculum development is a powerful instrument for change; it has the relevance and vitality created by being centred on the place where learner and teacher meet. Its ultimate success will depend not only on the quality of leadership within the school but on the teachers working within it. Positive implementation will depend on the capacity of these teachers to generate and above all manage and sustain innovation, and the appropriateness of their initial and in-service training to fit such a role.

Notes

1 Bullock Report, *A Language for Life*, London, HMSO, 1975.
2 P. Cloke (ed.), 'Language Across the Hele's Curriculum', Exeter, Hele's School, unpublished mimeo, 1977.
3 E. Hoyle, 'The creativity of the school in Britain', in A. Harris, M. Lawn and W. Prescott (eds), *Curriculum Innovation*, London, Croom Helm, 1974.
4 J. Nisbet, 1974, 'Innovation – bandwagon or hearse?', in ibid.
5 L. Stenhouse, 'Defining the Curriculum Problem'. Norwich, Centre for Applied Research in Education, unpublished mimeo, n.d.

Index

Abbs, P., 11
Abraham Moss Centre, 11, 58, 97–115
Advanced Physics Project for Independent Learning (ILEA), 22, 24–5, 39
Ashworth, P., 39

Beswick, N. W., 12, 58, 96
Biology Independent Resource Development, 25, 26
block timetabling, 61, 62, 66, 74–6, 82–4, 94, 117, 121–3
Bolam, R., 5, 13; see also Shipman, M. D.
Booth, P., see Reid, D. J.
Bosworth, D. P., 38
Bristol Achievement Test, 126, 131–3
Brown, M., 38; and McCullogh, D. J., 40
Bullock Report (1975), 91–3, 126, 134, 135, 144
Burden, I. J.: Howe, J. B. and Whittaker, M. J., 40; Turner, A. K. and Whittaker, M. J., 39

Certificate of Extended Education, 51
Children Investigating, 41, 42–3, 45–7, 51
Cloke, P., 11, 144

Clowne School Science Scheme, 28–9
Codsall School, 4, 10–11, 57–96
Computer Assisted Management of Learning in Physics, 25–8, 39
Cornwall Workshop, 39
Countesthorpe College, 14, 16, 38
curriculum development, 1–3, 4, 6, 15, 16, 17, 18, 20, 22, 33, 58, 59, 60, 79, 80, 82, 91, 94, 95; and examination system, 90–1
Curriculum Development Unit, 51

Department of Education and Science, 6, 13, 42
De Rose, J. V., 39
Dewey, J., 1

Eavis, P., 11
Eggleston, J., 12
Evans Integrated Themes, 42

Forward, R. W., 7, 12, 13
Foster, D., 39, 40
Frazer, M., 40

Gloucestershire ILIS Workshop Group, 29–31
Gonzales, G. M. de and Gilbert, J., 40
Grant, A. and Homan-Berry, P., 40

Green, A. G., *see* Sharp, R.
Green E. L., 10, 38, 39, 40
Green Paper (1977), 67, 96

Hannam, C., 132
Harlen, W., 34, 40
Harris, A., Lawn, M. and Prescott, W., 144
Hele's School, 11, 134–44
Herbert, P., 39, 40
Holder, M.: and Hewton, E., 12, 96; and Mitson, R., 96
Holt, M. J., 8, 13
Homan-Berry, P., 39; *see also* Grant, A.
Hoyle, E., 143, 144

independent learning, 14, 18, 19, 22, 24, 25, 30, 32, 33, 36, 37, 38, 99, 105
Independent Learning in Science, 10, 14–40; aims, 16–18; aims of teachers within, 18–20; evaluation of, 33–5; publications, 21, 32, 38; structure, 20–3
individualised learning, 2, 4, 8, 10, 28, 35, 78, 99, 105, 127
in-service training, 4–6, 11, 15, 58, 85–6, 94, 95, 96, 97, 98, 99–104, 106–14, 115, 118, 127, 131, 144

James Report, 4
Jenkins, D., *see* Shipman, M. D.

Lawn, M., *see* Harris, A.
Learning Through Science (Schools Council), 41–2
Leicestershire Education Authority, 21
Lewis, J., 39

McCullogh, D. J., 39; *see also* Brown, M.
Manor Park School, 11, 116–33
Medium Term Independent Learning in Physics, 39

Mitson, R., 11, 58, 62, 88, 96; *see also* Holder, M.
mixed ability, 2, 4, 29, 36–7, 60, 61, 66, 67, 76–9, 94, 95, 99, 106, 114, 117, 118, 123, 127, 131, 136, 142

Neill, A. S., 1
Newcastle Education Authority, 121, 127, 130
Nicholas, B., 39
Nisbet, J., 144
Nuffield: A-Level Physics Independent Learning Resources, 16; Combined Science (11–13) Project, 30, 41, 42, 45, 47; Foundation, 2–3, 4, 47; Integrated Science Project, 10; Junior Science, 42, 43; Science, 114; Working With Science Project, 41, 47–56

Partington, G., 4, 13
Pestalozzi, J. H., 1
Prescott, W., *see* Harris, A.

Queen Mary College, 48
Quest Project, 39

Reid, D. J. and Booth, P., 38
resource-based learning, 61–2, 83
resource centres/workshops, 9, 11, 15, 16, 17–18, 20–2, 38, 51, 58, 61–2, 78, 79, 82, 83, 84, 85–90, 94, 113, 119–20, 127–8, 130
Resource Centre Project (Schools Council), 4
Resources for Learning Project (Nuffield Foundation), 4
resources movement, 3–4
Rousseau, J.-J., 1

Salisbury workshop, 39
Schools and In-Service Teacher Education Evaluation Project (DES), 5

Schools Council, 2–3, 4, 16, 17,
    21, 34, 35, 91, 115; reports,
    6–7; working papers, 12, 13,
    39, 58
Schools Integrated Studies Project,
    3, 118
Science 5–13 Project (Schools
    Council), 10, 41, 42, 43–4, 45,
    47
Scottish Integrated Science, 42
secondment, 22–3
Shapland, J., 40; and Watson, P.,
    39
Sharp, R. and Green, A. G., 2, 12
Shipman, M. D., Bolam, D. and
    Jenkins, D., 3, 12
Skilbeck, M., 9, 12, 13
Staffordshire Education
    Authority, 51

Steers, N., 40
Stenhouse, L., 144

Tawney, D., 40
Taylor Report, 96
team teaching, 62, 66, 72, 83, 98,
    117–18, 119, 123
Temple, J., 39
Thames Valley College, 49
Turner, A. K., *see* Burden, I. J.

Walton, J., 82, 96; and Welton, J.,
    13
Waterhouse, P., 40
Watson, P., *see* Shapland, J.
White, J., 63, 96
Whitehead, J., 39, 40
Whittaker, M. J., *see* Burden, I. J.
Wild, K., 10
Wilson, M. D., 38, 39